Terry Pratchett's
Maskerade

Adapted for the stage by
Stephen Briggs

Samuel French — London
New York - Toronto - Hollywood

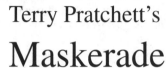

Terry Pratchett's
MASKERADE

First presented by the Studio Theatre Club at the Unicorn Theatre, Abingdon, on 14th November, 1995, with the following cast:

Granny Weatherwax	Laura Ridout
Nanny Ogg	Judith Leonard
Agnes Nitt	Sharon Stone
Walter Plinge	Nigel Tait
Mr Salzella	Stephen Briggs
Christine	Kath Leighton
Seldom Bucket	Trevor Collins
Dr Underschaft/Sgt Detritus	Tim Arnot
Señor Basilica	Mark Cowper
Greebo	Mike Davey
Mrs Plinge	Claire Spittlehouse
Mr Goatberger	Robin Allen
Mr Pounder/Cpl Nobbs	Graham Cook
Manager to Snr Basilica	Simon Banks
André	Andy Moseley
Colette	Sarah Salholm
Solange	Sarah Wilson
Giselle	Laima Bite
Hron	Martin Lyons
Kevin	John Kirchhoff
Mr Arno	Keith Franklin
Tommy Cripps	Simon Hill

Directed by Stephen Briggs
Lighting by Colin James
Stage Manager: Leonie Forman
Sound: Phil Evans and Gill Petrokofsky

CHARACTERS

Granny Weatherwax, *a witch*
Nanny Ogg, *another witch*
Agnes (Perdita) Nitt, *not a witch*
Walter Plinge, *a very odd-job man*
Dr Underschaft, *Chorus Master*
Mr Salzella, *Director of Music*
Mr Seldom Bucket, *Opera Manager*
Greebo, *a cat in human form*
Mrs Plinge, *Walter's mum*
Señor Enrico Basilica/Henry Slugg, *opera singer*
Christine, *opera star*
Mr Goatberger, *a publisher*
Tommy Cripps, *scenery painter*
Mr Pounder, *ratcatcher*
Snr Basilica's Manager
Death of Rats
André, *a pianist*
Sergeant Detritus, *City Watch, a troll*
Corporal Nobbs, *City Watch, a human?*
Arno, *the Stage Manager*
Hron, *a stagehand*
Kevin, *another stagehand*
Colette, *a dancer*
Solange, *another dancer*
Giselle, *also a dancer*
Corps de ballet, Stagecrew, Audience, Travellers, Bodies

AUTHOR'S INTRODUCTION

An Awfully Big Adventure

Oxford's Studio Theatre Club were the first people ever to dramatize the Discworld. That was in 1991, with *Wyrd Sisters*.

We had a theatre that seats ninety people. We had a stage about the size of a pocket handkerchief with the wings of Tinkerbell. Put on a Discworld play? Simple ...

A flat, circular world borne through space on the backs of four enormous elephants who themselves stand on the carapace of a cosmically large turtle? Nothing to it. A seven foot skeleton with glowing blue eyes? No problem. A sixty foot fire-breathing dragon? A cinch.

My drama club had already staged its own adaptations of other works: Monty Python's *Life of Brian* and *Holy Grail* — and Tom Sharpe's *Porterhouse Blue* and *Blott on the Landscape*. We were looking for something new when someone said, "Try Terry Pratchett — you'll like him."

So I ventured into the previously uncharted territory of the "Fantasy" section of the local bookstore. I read a Terry Pratchett book; I liked it. I read all of them. I wrote to Terry and asked if we could stage *Wyrd Sisters*. He said yes.

Wyrd Sisters sold out.

So did *Mort* the year after.

So did *Guards! Guards!*, *Men at Arms*, *Maskerade* and *Jingo* in the years after that. In fact, "sold out" is too modest a phrase. "Oversold very quickly so that by the time the local newspaper mentioned it was on we'd had to close the booking office" is nearer the mark.

My casts were all happy enough to read whichever book we were staging, and to read others in the canon too. The books stand on their own, but some knowledge of the wider Discworld ethos helps when adapting the stories, and can help the actors with their characterizations.

The Discworld stories are remarkably flexible in their character requirements. *Mort* has been performed successfully with a cast of three (adding in an extra thrill for the audience, who knew that sooner or later a character would have to have a dialogue with themselves. But it turned out very well). On the other hand, there is plenty of scope for peasants, wizards, beggars, thieves and general rhubarb merchants if the director is lucky enough to have actors available.

I'd better add a note of caution here. There are a lot of small parts in the plays which nevertheless require good acting ability (as we say in the Studio

Theatre Club: "There are no small parts, only small actors"). The character may have only four lines to say but one of them might well be the (potentially) funniest line in the play. Terry Pratchett is remarkably democratic in this respect. Spear-carriers, demons and even a humble doorknocker all get their moment of glory. Don't let them throw it away!

Terry writes very good dialogue. Not all authors do. But Terry, like Dickens, writes stuff which you can lift straight into your play. Although it was often necessary to combine several scenes from the book into one scene in the play, I tried to avoid changing the original Pratchett dialogue. After all, you perform an author's work because you like their style; as much of that style as possible should be evident in the play.

The important thing was to decide what was the basic plot: anything which didn't contribute to that was liable to be dropped in order to keep the play flowing. Favourite scenes, even favourite characters, had to be dumped.

I had to remember that not all the audience would be dyed-in-the-wool Pratchett fans. Some of them might just be normal theatre-goers who'd never read a fantasy novel in their whole lives, although I have to say that these now are a dwindling minority.

The books are episodic, and this can be a difficult concept to incorporate into a play. Set changes slow down the action. Any scene change that takes more than thirty seconds means you've lost the audience. Even ten-second changes, if repeated often enough, will lead to loss of interest.

The golden rule is — if you can do it without scenery, do it without scenery. It's a concept that has served radio drama very well (everyone knows that radio has the best scenery). And Shakespeare managed very well without it, too.

The plays do, however, call for some unusual props. Many of these were made by the cast and crew: a door with a hole for a talking golden door-knocker, coronation mugs, large hourglasses for Death's house, sponge chips and pizzas, shadow puppets, archaic rifles, dragon-scorched books and Discworld newspapers ("Patrician Launches Victim's Charter"). Other, more specialized props were put "out to contract": Death's sword and scythe, an orang-utan, the City Watch badge, a Death of Rats, a Greebo and two swamp dragons (one an elaborate hand puppet and one with a fire-proof compartment in its bottom for a flight scene).

Since the Studio Theatre Club started the trend in 1991, Terry and I have had many enquiries about staging the books — from as far afield as Finland, South Africa, Australia and the Czech Republic (as well as Sheffield, Aberdeen, Exeter and the Isle of Man).

So how did our productions actually go? We enjoyed them. Our audiences seemed to enjoy them (after all, some of them were prepared, year after year, to travel down to Abingdon in Oxfordshire from as far afield as Taunton, Newcastle-upon-Tyne, Ipswich, Basingstoke and ... well, Oxford). Terry seemed to enjoy them, too. He said that many of our members looked as though they had been recruited straight off the streets of Ankh-Morpork. He said that several of them were born to play the "rude mechanicals" in Vitoller's troupe in *Wyrd Sisters*. He said that in his mind's eye the famous Ankh-Morpork City Watch are the players of the Studio Theatre Club.

I'm sure these were meant to be compliments.

MASKERADE

By the time we staged *Maskerade* in 1995, we knew that the Discworld plays were a winner.

As with all the adaptations, there were difficult choices about which scenes should be sacrificed to try and keep the play down to a reasonable running time. We had also realized that Abingdon's medieval Unicorn Theatre was a part of the package; it has its shortcomings, but its ambience contributed much to the success of the shows. This, for us, would particularly be the case as it would itself easily play the part of the Ankh-Morpork City Opera House, in which most of the show takes place.

Maskerade had appealed to me for dramatization since Terry first mentioned the idea to me. The Phantom of the Opera theme is a strong one and he and I had fun researching backstage at the Royal Opera House, Covent Garden.

This dramatization was written with the Unicorn Theatre's restrictions, and the number of players I expected to have available, in mind. Really complicated scenic effects were virtually impossible. Basically, we had a bare stage with an onstage balcony at the back of the stage with a small curtained area beneath it. Anyone thinking of staging a Discworld play can be as imaginative as they like, calling upon the might of Industrial Light and Magic, if it's within their budget. But *Maskerade* can be staged with only a relatively modest outlay on special effects and the notes that accompany the text are intended to be a guide for those, like us, with limited budgets. Bigger groups, with teams of experts on hand, can let their imaginations run wild!

In short, though, our experience and that of other groups is that it pays to work hard on getting the costumes and lighting right, and to keep the scenery to little more than, perhaps, a few changes of level. One group with some resourceful technophiles achieved magnificent "scenery" simply with sound effects and lighting ("dripping water" and rippling green light for a dungeon scene, for example). There's room for all sorts of ideas here. The Discworld, as it says in the books, is your mollusc.

Characterization

Within the constraints of what is known and vital about each character, there is still room for flexibility of interpretation. With the main roles, though, you have to recognize that your audiences will expect them to look as much like the book descriptions as possible. *Maskerade* is, to an extent, easier in that few of the characters are Discworld "regulars". Also, most drama clubs don't have a vast range from which to choose and it's the acting that's more important than the look of the player when it comes down to it! There is some character description in the script notes, but here is a little more detail about the main protagonists.

Granny Weatherwax

In the opinion of many, not least herself, the greatest witch on the Discworld.

She is nominally the village witch of Bad Ass in the kingdom of Lancre in the Ramtops (a mountainous and unforgiving area of the Disc). For practical purposes, however, she regards the whole kingdom and, indeed, anywhere else she happens to be as her rightful domain.

She lives in the woods outside the village in a traditional, much-repaired witch's cottage, with beehives and a patch of what might be medicinal plants. She owns a broomstick, but despite the best efforts of dwarf engineers everywhere, it cannot be started without a considerable amount of running up and down with it in gear.

Esmerelda ("Granny") Weatherwax is a formidable character with every necessary attribute for the classical "bad witch" — a quick temper, a competitive, selfish and ambitious nature, a sharp tongue, an unshakeable conviction of her own moral probity, and some considerable mental and occult powers.

Granny likes to look the part. She is tall and thin, with blue eyes and with long, fine, grey hair tied back in a severe bun. She wears sensible black, her skirt incorporates some servicable pockets and her lace-up boots have complicated iron fixtures and toecaps like battering rams. She likes to wear several layers of clothing, including respectable flannelette petticoats. She wears a reinforced pointy hat, held in place by numerous hat-pins. She has perfect skin - a source of irritation; her compexion has resisted every one of her attempts to gain some warts.

Nanny Ogg

Gytha ("Nanny") Ogg is probably in her seventies. Her family arrangements are cosy but haphazard. She has been formally married three times. All three have passed happily, if somewhat energetically, to their well-earned rest. She has fifteen living children.

Contrary to the rules of traditional witchcraft Nanny Ogg now lives in quite a modern cottage in the centre of Lancre, with up-to-date conveniences like a modern wash copper and a tin bath a mere garden's walk away on a nail at the back of the privy. The cottage is between those of her sons Shawn and Jason. She likes to have all her family around her in case of an emergency, such as when she needs a cup of tea or the floor washed.

Nanny's hair is a mass of white curls. She is a small, plump, attractive and good-natured woman, with a crinkled face, thighs that could crack coconuts and a large and experienced bosom. She smokes a pipe and, like Granny Weatherwax, she wears heavy, lace-up boots.

Nobby

Corporal C W St J (Cecil Wormsborough St John) Nobbs. A Corporal in the Ankh-Morpork Night Watch. A four-foot tall, pigeon-chested, bandy-legged man, with the muscle tone of an elastic band and a certain resemblance to a chimpanzee. The only reason you can't say that Nobby is close to the animal kingdom is that the animal kingdom would move further away. Nobby is actually smaller than many dwarfs (er ... we compromised a bit on this!).

He is rumoured to have terrible personal habits, although these appear to be no more than a penchant for petty theft (usually from people too unconscious or, for preference, too dead to argue) an ability to do tricks with his facial boils, and a liking for folk dancing.

Men like Nobby can be found in any armed force. Although their grasp of the minutiae of the Regulations is usually encyclopaedic, they take good care never to be promoted beyond, perhaps, Corporal. He smokes incessantly, but the weird thing is that any cigarette smoked by Nobby becomes a dog-end almost instantly but remains a dog-end indefinitely or until lodged behind his ear, which is a sort of nicotine Elephants' Graveyard.

Nobby is known to have served as a quartermaster in the army of the Duke of Pseudopolis. There are rumours that he had to join the Watch after items missing from the stores were found in his kit. Since the items were the entirety of the store inventory, Nobby's kit at the time consisted of two warehouses.

Detritus

Detritus is a silicon-based life-form. A troll. There are lots of them in Ankh-Morpork. We had the good fortune to have already invested in a mask and gloves for our production of *Men at Arms*. He's only a minor character in this play, so you might just buy stuff from a fancy dress shop, or just use make-up.

The Phantom/Ghost

Discerning readers will notice that, throughout the play the masked man is called the "Ghost" by the characters in the script, but referred to by the adapter (me) as the "Phantom" in the stage directions. This inconsistency is simply that "Ghost" remains true to the book dialogue and reflects the characters' belief that the masked man is really supernatural. Whereas, to me, "Phantom", whilst still supernatural, is a more romantic title and is thus the one I used in the directions. After all — in the book by Gaston Leroux which has some parallels with Terry Pratchett's tale, Eric refers to himself in letters as "O.G." the Opera Ghost, but the "book" is called *The Phantom of the Opera*.

We had, in effect, three Phantoms. Each dressed, of course, identically. Two were Walter and Salzella. One, who we used only twice (I think) was just another member of the cast about the same build as our Walter and Salzella. This third Phantom was used in the first scene, to prevent either of the other two having too fast a costume change and, in one other scene, to give the impression that the "Walter Phantom" had jumped fifteen feet from a balcony. On the higher level, our Walter Phantom jumped from sight but it was the "double" who emerged a split second later at ground level. The stage notes make it clear which actor is playing the Phantom in each scene. This helps to involve the audience in the confusion that arises from identifying someone simply from their clothing and their white mask!

Costumes

We played most of the characters in a form of Victorian dress, though the men wore tights and buckle shoes instead of trousers. The City Watch were attired in uniforms of the English Civil War period, but with their opera cloaks, white ties and white waistcoats over the top of their armour.

We hired our outsize suit for Señor Basilica from Angel's and Berman's in London (from whom we also hired two identical opera cloaks for the various Ghosts).

Scenery

Virtually none. We had the chandelier hanging over the front of the audience throughout. It was made for the show and was wired to the lights and could be "rocked" from the wings by fine fishing wire, although the movement seemed to the audience to be caused by the actor shaking the thick supporting rope.

We also had a screen on stage for the Ghost's letters. Apart from that, there were just the odd bits of furniture, most of which were moved on and off stage by the "Opera's" stage crew.

Special Effects

Sword-stick and Sword-broom
We managed to hire a sword-stick from Bapty (the theatre armourers), but the sword-broom was made especially for the show — no, we don't still have it!

Stephen Briggs

ACT I
Scene 1
An Empty Stage

We are in the interior of the Ankh-Morpork Opera House. There is a theatre balcony with eight seats at the back of the stage with a small curtained area beneath it. (The curtains here will be referred to henceforth as "the small curtains".) Above the front few rows of the audience hangs an ornate chandelier with a faded glory; it is, as yet, unlit. To one side of the stage is a small screen on which the Phantom's letters will be projected

The overture starts and the house lights go down. In the complete Black-out, a cloaked and hatted figure (a double for the Phantom) moves around, carrying a lantern. He is wearing evening dress, with a black cloak, a broad-brimmed black hat and a white mask obscuring his face. As the overture ends, he is seen on the balcony, in a follow spot. He stands for a moment, then exits suddenly

The chandelier illuminates and the play begins. The music ends. On stage are some chorus people and stage crew, chatting. During the early part of the scene, Salzella, a tall, slim man in his forties, and Dr Underschaft enter the auditorium and stand at the back. (The auditorium mentioned here and henceforth is the actual auditorium in which the performance is taking place)

Walter Plinge enters, sweeping. He appears to be a gangling youth, wearing a long warehouseman's coat and a black beret. Almost immediately, Agnes Nitt enters DL on to the stage. She is a large girl in her early twenties, who would very much like to be a slim girl in her early twenties. She has a penchant for black lace

Agnes Nitt Excuse me.

The chorus people give her an uninterested glance. Walter Plinge jerks and drops the broom. He tries to pick it up and, in doing so, gets tangled in the broom handle and falls over. Agnes Nitt rushes to him to help him up

Oh, I'm so sorry! Are you all right?

Walter Plinge tries to get up and again gets tangled in the broom

Shall I hold the broom?

Agnes Nitt helps Walter Plinge to his feet

There. Do you work for the Opera House?
Walter Plinge Yes, miss!
Agnes Nitt Er, can you tell me where I go for the audition?
Walter Plinge Er, this is it, miss. You're here.

Mrs Plinge, Walter Plinge's mum, enters, carrying a box full of wine bottles

Hallo, Mum! (*To Agnes Nitt*) That's my mum.
Agnes Nitt Oh yes?
Walter Plinge Can I help you with those, Mum?
Mrs Plinge Oh Walter, would you? The delivery boy brought the drinks to the wrong entrance.

Mrs Plinge hands Walter Plinge the box. There is a bit of business as he tries to cope with the broom and the box

Er, I'll carry the broom, shall I?

Mrs Plinge and Walter Plinge exit. Mr Arno, the Stage Manager, enters with a clipboard

Arno Yes, miss?
Agnes Nitt Er ... I'm here for — the auditions. I, er, saw the notice that said you were auditioning today. Um, who was that?
Arno That's Walter. Walter Plinge. Everyone knows him. Now, miss — who are you?
Agnes Nitt Oh. I'm Ag — erm ... I'm Ag — er ... Perdita. Perdita X., er ... Nitt.
Arno Well, Perdita X Nitt, you're a bit early; we've only just finished the dress rehearsal for tonight's show. I'll just see if the Musical Director, Mr Salzella and the Chorus Master, Dr Underschaft, will hear you now. (*He looks out into the auditorium*)
Dr Underschaft (*from the auditorium*) Yes, very well, Mr Arno, as we're here.
Arno So – when you're ready.
Agnes Nitt Well, I've got this song. It's a ——
Arno Give us your music, then, and I'll give it to Miss Proudlet.
Agnes Nitt Er, there is no accompaniment, actually, it ——

Arno Oh, it's a folk song, is it? Blimey. Well, the best of luck, then.

Arno shuffles off

Salzella (*in the auditorium*) I don't think that we need to subject ourselves to a folk song, thank you, er, Perdita. Perhaps you would just sing us your scales?
Agnes Nitt Scales?
Salzella (*coming forward*) Yes. You know. "Doh-Re-Mi". Starting low and going up as high as you can? Thank you.

Agnes Nitt does a scale that stretches all the way from basso profundo to somewhere above dog-whistle

A number of corps de ballet and stage crew, including Christine, and Mr Arno, appear, attracted by this unusual audition. Christine is an attractive, slim, girl in her early twenties with bubbly blond hair and a personality to match. She seems always to talk in exclamations!!

At the zenith of Agnes Nitt's scale Salzella, followed by Dr Underschaft, walks on to the stage and a bat falls from the rafters

Dr Underschaft Is — is that your full range, my dear?
Agnes Nitt No.
Dr Underschaft No?
Agnes Nitt If I go any higher, people faint. And if I go any lower people say it makes them feel uncomfortable.

Dr Underschaft and Salzella whisper

I can sing with myself in thirds. You know, like doh-mi, but at the same time.
Dr Underschaft Splendid. Perhaps later. Now, your voice projection ——
Agnes Nitt Oh I can do that. Where would you like it projected?

Here the sound boffins must fix it so that Agnes Nitt's recorded voice can be moved around the speakers in the theatre!

(*From one speaker*) To here? (*To another*) Or here? (*To another*) Or here?

Salzella and Dr Underschaft look astounded

Salzella Well, erm, Perdita Nitt. You are now a member of the Ankh-Morpork City Opera chorus.

Salzella and Dr Underschaft move away

Christine You have an amazing voice! Hallo, I'm Christine! Isn't this exciting!?

Agnes Nitt Er, yes.

Christine I've waited all my life for this day. I trained with Mme Venturi at the Quirm Conservatory! Are you staying in the Opera tonight? What room are you in?

Agnes Nitt I don't know ...

Arno (*consulting his clipboard*) Well, you'd be in — number seventeen.

Christine Oh goody. Next to me. Do stay. Come on, let's look at our rooms!!

Agnes Nitt and Christine exit. Arno, the corps de ballet and stagehands drift off, too, leaving Underschaft and Salzella alone

Dr Underschaft Well. Now then, Salzella. What do you think of today's batch?

Seldom Bucket enters. He is a self-made man, in his fifties

Ah, Mr Bucket. We were just considering today's batch of auditionees.

Seldom Bucket Yes, Dr Underschaft. I watched most of the audition from the gods. That Christine. Marvellous stage presence, eh? Good figure, too. (*He winks at Dr Underschaft*)

Dr Underschaft Yes. Very pretty. I'm still not happy about you hiring her, though. She can't sing.

Seldom Bucket What you artistic types don't seem to realize is that this is the Century of the Fruitbat. Opera is a production, not just a load of songs. The idea that a soprano should have fifteen acres of bosom and a horned helmet belongs to the past, like.

Salzella and Underschaft exchange glances

Salzella Unfortunately, the idea that a soprano should have a reasonable singing voice does not belong to the past. She has a good figure, yes. She has a certain ... sparkle. She'll look good on stage. But she can't sing.

Seldom Bucket You can train her, can't you? After a few years in the chorus?

Dr Underschaft Yes, maybe after a few years, if I persevere, she will merely be very bad.

Seldom Bucket Er, gentlemen. Ahem. All right. Cards on the table, yes? I'm a simple man, me. No beating about the bush, speak as you find, call a spade a spade.

Salzella Do give us your forthright views.

Seldom Bucket I've been through the mill, I have. And I made myself what I am today ——

Salzella Self-raising flour?

Seldom Bucket — but I do have to, er, declare a bit of a financial interest. Her dad did in fact, er, lend me a fair whack of money to help me to buy this place. And he made a heartfelt plea on behalf of his daughter. Um. If I remember correctly, it was "Don't make me have to break your legs". I don't expect you artistes to understand. It's a business thing.

Salzella Very well. It's your opera house, I'm sure. Now Perdita ...?

Dr Underschaft I'm sure she will prove an asset.

Seldom Bucket Yes, what a range she's got.

Salzella Yes, I saw you staring.

Seldom Bucket I meant her voice, Salzella. She will add body to the chorus.

Salzella Ye-e-es. But could you ever see her in a major role?

Seldom Bucket Heck, no. Wonderful personality. though. And good hair, of course. So we will keep them both on, then. Mmmm?

Salzella
Underschaft } (*together*) Yes. Yes I suppose we will.

They exit

The Phantom (the double) appears on the balcony, watching them

The Lights cross-fade to:

SCENE 2
The Blasted Heath

The small curtain opens. Wind noise. Thunder. Lightning. Smoke billows out over the stage. We see that there is a small "fire" on stage

Granny Weatherwax and Nanny Ogg are invisible in the smoke. Granny Weatherwax is tall and slim, with a determined expression. Nanny Ogg is short and dumpy, with a large, comfortable bosom. Both are in their sixties to seventies

Nanny Ogg (*in the fog*) When shall we — two meet again?

Granny and Nanny appear through the fog, Granny striding through purposefully, Nanny breezing in fanning at the "fog" with her hands. They both carry toasting forks

Granny Weatherwax For goodness' sake, Gytha. What on earth did you have to go and shout that for?

Nanny Ogg Sorry, Esme. I was just doing it for, you know — old times' sake. Don't roll off the tongue, tho'.

Granny Weatherwax You made me drop me toast on the fire.

Nanny Ogg Sorry.

Granny Weatherwax Anyway, you didn't have to shout.

Nanny Ogg Sorry.

Granny Weatherwax I mean, I ain't deaf. You could've asked me in a normal voice. And I'd 'ave said, next Wednesday. Pass me another slice.

Nanny Ogg Magrat! Pass us the bre — oh. Whoops, mind wandering for a minute there. I'll get it.

Granny Weatherwax Hah!

Nanny Ogg I thought it might cheer you up. Comin' up here again.

Granny Weatherwax Really.

Nanny Ogg Take you out of yourself, sort of thing.

Granny Weatherwax Hmf.

Nanny Ogg Um. Erm. Now — look here, Esme. Look, I'm worried, see. Er, about, um, you. Very worried. I don't want to think that you might be turning — "black"?

Granny Weatherwax "Black"?

Nanny Ogg I know it can happen, with the really powerful witches. And let's face it, Esme, you're pretty damn powerful. Prob'ly even more than — Black Allis. And ev'ryone knows what happened to her.

Granny Weatherwax Yes yes. Stuffed into her own stove by a couple of kids. Good job too, to my mind. Even if it did take a week to clean the oven. Anyway, I ain't going "black".

Nanny Ogg Ah. (*Pause*) Saw Magrat the other day.

No reaction

She's looking well. Queening suits her.

No reaction

Don't think she's missin' being the third member of our coven one little bit. (*Pause*) The Maiden, the Mother and the Crone, eh? Well, I reckon it's safe to assume that ole Magrat no longer qualifies as the maiden nowadays — but I've still got me fifteen kids and — er ...

Granny Weatherwax Yes, well. Is that tea ready, Gytha?

Nanny Ogg goes back to the fire to pick up two mugs of tea. She hands one to Esme and downs hers quite quickly

Nanny Ogg What about that Agnes Nitt?

Granny Weatherwax What? Perditax?

Nanny Ogg Perdita X.

Granny Weatherwax She showed some promise, I 'spose. Might do as the third witch at a pinch.

Nanny Ogg Nope. Nearly forgot. Saw her mum the other day. She's gone off to Ankh-Morpork. Had some idea about joining the Opera.

Granny Weatherwax Opera? What's that?

Nanny Ogg Well, it's a bit like theatre, but with more singing and less acting.

Granny Weatherwax Less acting? Less acting than theatre? How do they manage that? Can't see Agnes Nitt — Perdita — fitting in too well. She's a sensible girl. Not flighty like them actresses we seen.

Nanny Ogg She said Lancre was dull, her mum said.

Granny Weatherwax Dull?

Nanny Ogg That's what I said. I said we get some lovely sunsets up here. And there's the annual fair every Soul Cake Tuesday. Regular. (*She finishes her tea and peers into her mug*) Bleeding bloody hell!

Granny Weatherwax What's up? No sugar?

Nanny Ogg Look! Esme, look!

Nanny Ogg hands the mug to Granny Weatherwax

And think of Agnes when you do.

Granny Weatherwax (*hissing between her teeth*) Well, well. There's a thing.

Nanny Ogg Do you see it?

Granny Weatherwax Yes. A shape. Like a skull.

Nanny Ogg And them eyes? I bloody near pi — I was pretty damn surprised I can tell you. She could be facing something bad, Esme. Her mum giv me one of her letters home — here. (*She reaches into her pocket. A big wodge of letters falls out*)

Granny Weatherwax Hallo. What's all this, then? (*She picks up some of the letters*) "The Lancre Witch"? Why've you got my post in your pocket, Gytha? And why're people writing to me? (*She opens one; reading*) "Dear Lancre Witch, I would just like to say how much I appreciated the Carrot and Oyster Pie. My husband ... " (*Her voice trails off. She looks incredulous and angry*)

Nanny Ogg starts to exit, sideways

Gytha Ogg, you stay right here! (*She opens another couple of letters and skims them*)

Nanny Ogg Thing is, my late husband said to me once, after dinner, he said, "You know, Mother, it'd be a real shame if all them recipes you know just

passed away when you did." So I started to scribble stuff down, as and
when. Then I thought it might be nice to have it done properly so I sent it
off to the almanack people in Ankh-Morpork and they hardly charged me
anything at all, and a while later they sent me this ... (*She pulls out a book*)
It's amazing how they get the letters so neat ...

Granny Weatherwax You done a book.

Nanny Ogg Only cookery.

Granny Weatherwax (*taking the book and reading the cover*) "The Joye
of Snacks. Bye a Lancre Witche".

Nanny Ogg It's my gnome de plum. The almanack man — Mr Goatberger
— said it'd make it sound more mysterious.

Granny Weatherwax (*reading*) "One hundred and twenty-third Prynting.
More Than Twentie Thousande Sold. One Half Dollar". You sent them
money to get them printed?

Nanny Ogg Only a couple of dollars. Then they sent the money back
afterwards, only they got it wrong and sent three dollars. So I kept quiet
about it. Di'n't want him saying he wanted it back.

Granny Weatherwax Oh, yes.

Nanny Ogg After all, money's not important, is it?

Granny Weatherwax Good. 'Cos I reckon this Mr Goatberger owes you
a bit more than you got, if there's any justice.

Nanny Ogg Oh?

Granny Weatherwax About four or five thousand dollars, I should think.
(*Pause*) So it's a good job money don't matter. It'd be terrible otherwise.
All that money, matterin'.

Nanny Ogg What?

Granny Weatherwax Could be a bit more. Beats me why anyone'd fall over
themselves to buy a cookery book, though ... It is a cookery book, isn't it?

Nanny Ogg Oh yes. Recipes. And, er — cookery anecdotes. Um. Look
under "Famous Carrot and Oyster Pie." Page twenty-five.

Esme turns to page twenty-five of the book

And — er — "Cinnamon and Marshmallow Fingers" — page seventeen.
Er — there's "Humorous Puddings and Cake Decoration". That's all of
Chapter Six. What one you looking at?

Granny Weatherwax (*reading; pointedly*) "Strawberry Wobbler." (*Pause*)
Gytha. This is me asking this. Is there any page in this book which does not
relate in some way to — er — goings on? What about this one? (*She reads*)
"Maids of Honour"?

Nanny Ogg Ah. Well they starts off as Maids of Honour. But they ends up
as Tarts.

Granny Weatherwax (*reading*) "A Witch of Lancre".

Nanny Ogg Sorry, Esme.

Granny Weatherwax People'll think that's me.

Nanny Ogg Yes, Esme.

Granny Weatherwax It's got to be changed.

Nanny Ogg Yes, Esme.

Granny Weatherwax We're going to see your Mr Goatberger, Gytha. He's going to put a stop to this. I can't have people looking at me and thinking about "Bananana Soup Surprise".

Nanny Ogg No, Esme.

Granny Weatherwax And I'll come with you to make sure you do.

Nanny Ogg Yes, Esme.

Granny Weatherwax And we'll talk to the man about your money. And we might just drop in on young Agnes to make sure she's all right.

Nanny Ogg Yes, Esme.

Granny Weatherwax But we'll do it diplomatic-like. Don't want people saying I'm interfering. You won't find anyone calling me a busybody.

Nanny Ogg Yes, Esme.

Granny Weatherwax That was, "Yes, Esme, you won't find anyone calling you a busybody", was it?

Nanny Ogg Oh, yes, Esme.

Granny Weatherwax Good. Right. Come on then.

Granny Weatherwax strides away and exits

Nanny Ogg Now this is more like it!

The small curtains close. The Lights cross-fade to:

Scene 3
The Opera House

Christine and Agnes Nitt walk on to the stage in front of the small curtains

Christine ... and then I said "No!". I won't do it! This (*she describes her dress*) dress will do splendidly for the audition! But enough about me. What about you? Tell me all about yourself! You're so lucky. You have such a majestic figure for opera! Black suits you by the way!

Agnes Nitt Er — well — I'm from somewhere up in the mountains that you've probably never heard of ——

Christine And have you seen the mirror in my room? It's huge! Apparently it's built into the wall!

Agnes Nitt — and my father is the King of Lancre and my mother is a small tray of raspberry puddings.

Christine That's interesting. You have a lovely personality, you know.

Agnes Nitt You know, I woke up one morning realizing that I'd been saddled with "a lovely personality". No-one ever asked me if I'd prefer a lovely personality or a body that'd take a size eight in dresses. I got a reputation for being capable in a crisis. Next thing you know I'd have been making shortbread and apple pies and then there'd be no hope. So, I thought — I'd be Perdita. Use black notepaper. Be pale and mysterious. I mean, were the witches really the only alternative? I knew I had some occult talent. Sometimes I'd know that a thing was about to happen. But I've seen the way the witches live. Nanny Ogg's all right, but Granny Weatherwax? Oh yes. Finest job in the world? Being a sour old woman with no friends? No thank you! I've always liked singing. I'm good at singing. So — I came here.

Christine Do you think my hair looks all right?

Agnes Nitt Oh. Yes, it ... What was that? I thought I heard someone — up there!

Christine It's probably the Ghost!! We've got one, you know.

Agnes Nitt A man with his face covered with a white mask.

Christine Oh. You've heard about him, then? They say he watches every performance, from Box Eight! They say if anyone ever sits in Box Eight, there'll be a dreadful tragedy! Isn't it romantic?

The chandelier sways slightly

Agnes Nitt That looks like an accident waiting to happen, if ever I saw one.

There is a horrible scream off stage

Colette, some of the chorus, and Mrs Plinge rush on

It came from off stage!

Voice (*off*) Open the tabs!

The small curtains open. There is a body on the floor. It is Tommy Cripps. The Phantom (Salzella, unrecognizable to the audience) stands next to him and runs off as soon as the curtains open. Several of the chorus girls scream again

Colette (*crossing to the body*) It's blood!

Christine Blood! It's blood! Blood!!

Agnes Nitt (*crossing to the body*) It's turpentine. Shouldn't we help him up?

Agnes Nitt helps Tommy up

Mrs Plinge It's Tommy Cripps. He paints scenery.

Tommy moans and opens his eyes

Tommy Cripps I saw him! It was horrible!
Agnes Nitt Saw what?

Voices in the crowd mutter

Giselle Marie-Claire says she saw him last week!
Solange He's here! It's happening again!
Christine Are we all doomed?!
Tommy Cripps (*gripping Agnes Nitt's arm*) He's got a face like death!
Agnes Nitt Who?
Tommy Cripps The Ghost! It's white bone! He has no nose!
Agnes Nitt He has no nose? Then how does he smell?

> *Mr Pounder enters, speaking as he does so. Pounder wears a tatty tailcoat and top hat. He is carrying a sack, which moves around, as if it contains a living thing*

Mr Pounder I saw him too! No nose!
Agnes Nitt Yes, but if he has no nose, how does he ——
Mr Pounder (*crossing the stage to the crowd*) I saw him! Ooooh yes! Wi' his great black cloak and his white face with no eyes but only two holes where his eyes should be. Ooooh! And ...
Agnes Nitt He had a mask on?
Mr Pounder (*glaring at Agnes Nitt*) And he had no nose!
Tommy Cripps I just said that. I told them that. They already know that.
Agnes Nitt Yes, but if he had no nose, how did he sme ——
Mr Pounder Did you mention the eyes?
Agnes Nitt Are we talking about some kind of mask here?

The crowd all turn and look at Agnes Nitt

Tommy Cripps He jumped out from behind the organ. Next thing I knew, there was this rope around my neck.

Salzella sweeps in

Salzella All right, everyone. What's going on here? Mr Pounder?
Mr Pounder I knows what I saw, Mr Salzella. I see lots of things, I do.
Salzella As much as is visible through the bottom of a bottle I have no doubt, you old reprobate. What happened to Tommy?
Tommy Cripps (*pleased to have centre stage again*) It was the Ghost! He swooped out at me, Mr Salzella! Er, I think my leg is broken! (*He limps a bit*)

Salzella Back again, is he? Dear me. Some of you help Tommy down to the canteen. And someone else fetch a doctor ...

Agnes Nitt His leg isn't broken. But that's a nasty rope burn on his neck, and he's filled his ear with paint.

Tommy Cripps What do you know about it, miss?

Agnes Nitt I've, er, had some training.

Salzella Yes. Thank you, Perdita. Come along now, everyone, on with your work.

Everyone except Salzella moves to exit, some of the chorus helping Tommy

Not you, Christine, and Perdita.

Christine and Agnes Nitt stop

Tommy Cripps (*as he goes*) Take me to the canteen, Mr Salzella said. I've had a shock. What I need is a nice mug of sweet tea and a couple of cheese rolls ...

Tommy exits, with assistance

Mr Pounder (*trying to regain his position as Ghost expert; as he goes*) Big dark holes. Big ones.

Mr Pounder exits

Salzella Yes, thank you, Mr Pounder. (*He turns to the girls*) Did you see anything?

Christine I saw a creature with great flapping wings and great big holes where his eyes should be.

Agnes Nitt I'm afraid I just saw something white. Sorry.

Salzella You mean you see things that are really there? I can see you haven't been in the opera long, my dear. It's a pleasure to have a level-headed person around here for once. Observant and level-headed. Whereas I can see that you, Christine, will fit right in here.

André enters. He is a tall, slim young man

André, what is it?

André Someone's been smashing the organ, Mr Salzella. The pallet springs and the backfalls and everything.

Salzella All right. I'll tell Mr Bucket. Thank you.

Salzella strides off

Black-out

Scene 4
On The Road Near Bad Ass

Granny Weatherwax and Nanny Ogg enter into a tight spotlight. They both have broomsticks and bags, but Nanny is also carrying a sturdy-looking cat box big enough to hold the human Greebo later on. They stand for a moment, Nanny looking bright and cheery, Granny looking cross

Granny Weatherwax It's late.

Nanny Ogg Yep. It always is.

Granny Weatherwax Don't see why we couldn't go by broom.

Nanny Ogg 'S too draughty this time of year, Esme. The breeze gets into places I wouldn't dream of talking about.

Granny Weatherwax Really? Can't think where they'd be, then.

Nanny Ogg Oh Esme!

Granny Weatherwax Don't "Oh Esme" me! It weren't me that come up with the "Amusing Wedding Trifle with Special Sponge Fingers".

Nanny Ogg Anyway, Greebo don't like it on the broomstick. He's got a delicate stomach.

Granny Weatherwax Gytha, I've seen him eat half a skunk, so don't talk to me about delicate stomachs. (*Pause*) Anyway, he's been doing *It* again. He did *It* in ole Mrs Grope's henhouse last week. She had to have a lie down.

We hear a stagecoach approaching

Nanny Ogg He only does *It* when he's really in a corner. It was your fault, really, Esme; you changed him into a man when we was fighting your wicked sister. He never really got over it. He was prob'ly more frightened than Gladys Grope was, if truth be told. Ah. Here's the coach. (*She waves her arms*)

We hear the coach stop

Two tickets to Ankh-Morpork, please.

Coachman (*off*) What do you mean? The coach doesn't stop here!

Nanny Ogg Looks stopped to me.

Coachman (*off*) Listen, lady, even if I was stopping here the tickets are forty damn dollars each.

Nanny Ogg Oh.

Coachman (*off*) Here, hang about. Why have you two got broomsticks? Are you witches?

Nanny Ogg Yes. Have you got any special low terms for witches?

Coachman (*off*) Yeah, how about meddling, interfering old baggages?

Nanny and Granny exchange glances. They nod

Granny Weatherwax Er, young man, I wonder if I might just have a word with you?

Black out. In the dark, we hear an agonized cry. When the Lights come up, Nanny and Granny are sitting in the stagecoach, represented by chairs (think of the car scene in "The Rocky Horror Show", or the one in "Red Dwarf; Back to Reality"). Opposite them sit three travellers, one of whom is Enrico Basilica, a man of Pavarotti dimensions! Another is his Manager. A further passenger sits next to Gytha

Nanny Ogg You shouldn't ort to do that to people, Esme. (*She looks around the coach*) Morning. I see we've all opted to travel inside then? I'm Gytha Ogg and this is my friend Granny Weatherwax. We're going to Ankh-Morpork. Would anyone like an egg sandwich? I've brung plenty. The cat's bin sleeping on them, but they'll bend back OK. No? Please yourself, I'm sure. Let's see what else we've got ... Ah, has anyone got an opener for a bottle of beer?

One of the passengers hands Nanny a bottle opener

Fine. Now, anyone got anything to drink a bottle of beer out of?

Another passenger indicates that they have glasses or cups

Good. Now, has anybody got a bottle of beer?

Black-out

Scene 5
Mr Bucket's Office at the Opera House

Seldom Bucket sits at his desk, frowning at some ledgers. Tea things are in evidence. There is a knock at the door

Seldom Bucket Come in.

Salzella enters

Ah, Salzella, thank you for coming. You don't know who Q is, by any chance?

Salzella No, Mr Bucket.

Seldom Bucket Or R?

Salzella I'm afraid not.

Seldom Bucket It's taken me all morning, trying to make sense of these books. So much of the record is just on scraps of paper. "I've taken thirty dollars to pay Q. See you Monday, R." What the hell does it all mean?

Salzella I'm sure I couldn't say.

Seldom Bucket Do you know we pay more than fifteen hundred dollars a year for ballet shoes alone?

Salzella Yes, they do rather go through them at the toes.

Seldom Bucket It's ridiculous! I've still got a pair of boots that belonged to my father!

Salzella Yes, but ballet shoes, sir, are more like foot gloves.

Seldom Bucket You're telling me! They cost seven dollars a pair and only last for a few performances. There must be some way to make savings!

Salzella Perhaps we could ask the girls to spend more time in the air? A few extra *grand jetés*?

Seldom Bucket Would that work?

Salzella Actually, it was another matter about which I came to see you.

Seldom Bucket Oh?

Salzella It's to do with the organ we had. Someone has smashed it.

Seldom Bucket Who?

Salzella Tell me. When Mr Cavaille and Mr Pigneus sold you this opera house, did they mention anything — supernatural?

Seldom Bucket Oh yes. They did make some jokey remark about something, I think. They said, um, "Oh and by the way there's some man in evening dress who haunts the place, haha, ridiculous isn't it, these theatrical people, like children really, haha, but you may find it keeps them happy if you always keep Box Eight free on first nights, haha." I remember that quite well. Handing over thirty thousand dollars concentrates the mind a bit. And then they rode off. Quite a fast carriage, now I come to think about it.

Salzella Ah. well, now that the ink is dry, I wonder if I might fill you in on the fine detail. There's this Ghost. Every time anyone loses a hammer in this place, it's the Ghost. Every time someone cracks a note, it's because of the Ghost. On the other hand, every time someone finds a lost object, it's because of the Ghost. Every time someone has a good scene, it must be because of the Ghost. Every so often someone sees him — albeit fleetingly. We let him use Box Eight free on every first night performance.

Seldom Bucket And you say people like him?

Salzella Like is rather a strong word for it. It would be more correct to say that ... Well, it's pure superstition, of course, but they think he's lucky. Thought he was, anyway.

Seldom Bucket (*flatly*) Lucky.

Salzella Luck is important. I imagine that luck was not an important factor in the cheese business?

Seldom Bucket We used to rely on rennet. Look, you said "thought he was" lucky. What happened?

Salzella There have been — accidents.

Seldom Bucket What kind of accidents?

Salzella The kind of accidents that you prefer to call — accidents.

Seldom Bucket Oh. Like the time that Reg Plenty and Fred Chiswell were working late one night up on t' curdling vats and it turned out that Reg had been seeing Fred's wife and somehow, er, somehow he must have tripped, Fred said, and fallen ...

Salzella I am not familiar with the gentlemen concerned but — that kind of accident. Yes.

Seldom Bucket That were some of the finest Farmhouse Nutty that we ever made. (*Pause*) Now, what about these accidents?

Salzella A seamstress stitched herself to the wall. A deputy stage manager was found stabbed with a prop sword. Oh, and you wouldn't like me to tell you what happened to the man who worked the trapdoor. And all the lead mysteriously disappeared from the roof, although personally I don't think that was the work of the Ghost. The Ghost likes to leave little messages. There was one today by the remains of the organ. A scenery painter spotted him and ... nearly had an accident.

Salzella produces a note and hands it to Bucket. The note appears on the screen:
   "*Ahahahahahahaha! Ahahaha! Ahaha! BEWARE!!!!!*
   Yrs sincerely,The Opera Ghost"

What sort of person sits down and writes a maniacal laugh? And all those exclamation marks, you notice? Five? A sure sign of a man who wears his underpants on his head. Opera can do that to a man. Look, at least let's search the building. The cellars go on forever and we'll need a boat, of course...

Seldom Bucket A boat? In the cellar? No, they didn't tell me about the sub-basement. They were too busy not telling me that someone goes around killing the company. No-one said "By the way, people are dying a lot, and there's rising damp in the cell ——"

Salzella They're flooded. Didn't you have a look?

Seldom Bucket They said the cellars were fine!

Salzella And you believed them.

Seldom Bucket Well, there was rather a lot of champagne...

Salzella sighs

Look, I pride myself on being a good judge of character, and ... oh blast!

Señor Enrico Basilica will be here shortly. I can't risk anything happening to such a great star. Do you think he'll be all right?

Salzella Cut throat, perhaps.

Seldom Bucket What? Do you think so?

Salzella How should I know?

Seldom Bucket What should I do? Close the place? It hardly seems to make any money as it is! Why hasn't anyone told the City Watch?

Salzella That would be worse. Big trolls in rusty chain mail tramping everywhere, getting in everyone's way and asking stupid questions.

Seldom Bucket Oh we can't have that. Can't have them ... putting everyone on edge.

Salzella On edge? This is opera, Mr Bucket. Everyone is always on edge. Have you ever heard of a catastrophe curve?

Seldom Bucket Well, I know there's a dreadful bend in the road up by ——

Salzella A catastrophe curve, Mr Bucket, is what opera runs along. Opera happens because a large number of things amazingly fail to go wrong. It works because of hatred and love and nerves. All the time. This isn't cheese, this is opera. If you wanted a quiet retirement, Mr Bucket, you shouldn't have bought the Opera House. You should have gone into something peaceful, like alligator dentistry.

Seldom Bucket Now look. I may just be a big man in cheese to you. You may think I wouldn't know culture if I found it floating in me tea, but I have been a patron of the opera for many years.

There is a series of random knocks on the door

Salzella Come in, Walter.

Walter Plinge enters

You may have seen a lot of opera, but what do you know of production?

Walter Plinge I've just come to take away the tea things, Mr Bouquet.

Walter clatters away during all this, clumsily removing the tea things

Seldom Bucket Bucket! (*To Salzella*) I've been behind the scenes in lots of theatres ...

Salzella Oh theatre. Theatre doesn't even approach it. Opera isn't theatre with singing and dancing, you know. Opera's opera. The singers all loathe the sight of each other, the chorus hate the dancers, the prompt-side staff won't talk to the opposite-prompt staff. And that's only the start of it ...

Seldom Bucket Good grief! And I thought it was tough in cheese! I paid thirty thousand for this place. It's in the centre of the city! Prime site. I thought it was hard bargaining! Look, how does the Ghost get into this Box Eight I'm supposed to keep free for him?

Salzella No-one knows. We've searched and searched for secret entrances.

Seldom Bucket Does he pay?

Salzella shakes his head

But it's worth fifty dollars a night!

Salzella There will be trouble if you sell it.

Seldom Bucket Good grief, you're an educated man! Some creature in a mask has the run of the place, gets a prime box all to himself, kills people and you sit there and say there'll be trouble?

Salzella The show must go on.

Seldom Bucket Why? We never said the cheese must go on!

Salzella Yes, but the power of the show, the soul of the show, all the effort that's gone into it — it leaks out and spills everywhere.

Seldom Bucket But what about these accounts? Who does the book-keeping?

Salzella We all do, I suppose. Money gets put in; money gets taken out. Is it important?

Seldom Bucket Important?

Salzella Because — opera doesn't make money. Opera never makes money. Cheese makes money. Opera is what you spend that money on.

Seldom Bucket But what do I get out of it?

Salzella You get opera. You put in money, and you get out opera.

Seldom Bucket There's no profit?

Salzella Profit? Profit? No, I don't believe I've come across the word.

Seldom Bucket I mean, I knew the place wasn't making much, but I thought that was because it was being run badly. We have big audiences! We charge a mint for tickets! Now I'm told that a Ghost runs around killing people and we don't even make any money!!

Salzella Ah, opera!

Black-out

SCENE 6
On the Stagecoach

Granny and Nanny are now alone in the coach with Enrico Basilica, who is asleep

Nanny Ogg Certainly an interesting way to travel. You do get to see places.

Granny Weatherwax Yes. About every five miles, it seems to me.

Nanny Ogg Can't think what's got into me. I think it was that beer on top
of them egg sandwiches. 'Ow come everyone else is travelling up top,
now?

Granny Weatherwax I wouldn't be surprised if Greebo didn't have
something to do with that. None of 'em knew where that godsawful smell
of fermenting carpets was coming from, Gytha, but they knew where it was
going.

They joggle along for a while

Coachman (*off*) Look out! Potholes.

*In the coach, the three occupants bounce up and down as the coach goes over
the potholes. Nanny Ogg stares at Enrico Basilica*

Nanny Ogg Wouldn't like to come between him and his pudding.

Granny Weatherwax continues to stare out of the window

Granny Weatherwax Gytha?
Nanny Ogg Yes, Esme?
Granny Weatherwax Mind if I ask you a question? If your house was on
fire, what's the first thing you'd try to take out?
Nanny Ogg This is one of them personality questions, ain't it? You try and
guess what I'm like by what I say ...
Granny Weatherwax Gytha Ogg, I've known you all me life, I knows what
you're like, I don't need to guess. But answer me, all the same.
Nanny Ogg I reckon I'd take Greebo.

Granny Weatherwax nods

'Cos that shows I've got a warm and considerate nature.
Granny Weatherwax No, it shows that you're the kind of person who tries
to work out what the right answer's supposed to be. Untrustworthy. That
was a witch's answer if ever I heard one.
Nanny Ogg Oh. Thank you very much, Esme.
Enrico Basilica (*snoring loudly; talking in his sleep*) Treacle pudding, with
lots of custard ...
Nanny Ogg That reminds me. I'm a bit peckish. How about you, Esme? I
got a bit of pork pie in me bag.

Enrico Basilica wakes

'Ow about you, mister? Bit of pork pie?

Enrico Basilica Ooh, delicious. If I may, if I may. I haven't tasted pork pie in ages.

Nanny Ogg Beer?

Enrico Basilica Temptress! I'm not supposed to have beer. Wrong ambience. They don't allow it.

Nanny Ogg They?

Enrico Basilica Don't tell anyone, will you? You've made a friend of Henry Slugg.

Granny Weatherwax And what do you do, Henry Slugg?

Enrico Basilica I'm — I'm on the stage.

Nanny Ogg Yeah. we can see that.

Enrico Basilica No, no. I meant — we're slowing down.

Nanny Ogg (*peering out*) Yep. Sto Lat. Last overnight stop before Ankh-Morpork.

Voice 1 (*off*) Sto Lat! Sto Lat!

Voice 2 (*off*) Everyone off the coach, please.

Nanny Ogg Come on, Esme.

Black-out

SCENE 7
The Opera House

It is dark on stage. In the shadows is the dark-clad figure of André, carrying a dark lantern

Agnes Nitt enters, wearing a business-like nightie and dressing-gown and carrying a glass of water and a lighted candle. Suddenly, she hears a noise

Agnes Nitt Who's there?

André opens the door in his dark lantern and Agnes Nitt is illuminated by a square of yellow light

André Who's that? Oh. It's — Perdita, isn't it?

Agnes Nitt André? What are you doing there?

André I was — looking at the place where the Ghost tried to strangle Tommy Cripps.

Agnes Nitt Why?

André I, er, wanted to make sure that everything was safe, now, of course.

Agnes Nitt Didn't the stagehands do that?

André Oh, you know them. I just thought I'd better make certain. But what are you doing up and about?

Agnes Nitt Oh, I had to come down to get a glass of water for Christine. She didn't want to come all the way down to the pump by herself.

André Oh yes. Some of you girls have bedrooms in the building, don't you?
Well, I'll leave you to your errand. Good-night.
Agnes Nitt Good-night, André.

André exits

That's stupid. He was on stage this morning. No-one could move that
fast ...

Christine enters, wearing a floaty nightdress and carrying a lighted candle

Christine Perdita!?
Agnes Nitt Christine? What is it?
Christine I wondered where you'd got to! I was frightened!
Agnes Nitt What of?
Christine The big mirror in my room! It talked to me!! Can I sleep in your
room!?
Agnes Nitt Your mirror talked to you?
Christine Yes!
Agnes Nitt Oh well. One bed is much like another, I suppose. Come on, then.

*Christine and Agnes Nitt exit. As they do so, the small curtains open to
reveal Christine's room, with its bed and the large mirror*

Agnes Nitt enters and gets into bed

There is a "ting" from a tuning fork

*We hear the voice of the Phantom from off stage; it is, in fact, Walter's voice,
disguised*

The Phantom (*off*) Christine — please attend.
Agnes Nitt Yes?! Who's there?!
The Phantom (*off*) A friend.
Agnes Nitt In the middle of the night?!
The Phantom (*off*) Night is nothing to me. I belong to the night. And I can
help you.
Agnes Nitt Help me to do what?!
The Phantom (*off*) Don't you want to be the best singer in the opera?
Agnes Nitt Oh, Agnes is a lot better than me!!
The Phantom (*off*) But while I cannot teach her to look and move like you,
I can teach you to sing like her. Tomorrow you will sing the part of Iodine.
But I will teach you how to sing it perfectly ——

The Lights fade to Black-out

SCENE 8
In The Inn At Sto Lat

A bed US, *and the cat box, from which the human Greebo must be capable of appearing* (*perhaps over a trapdoor, or resting on a trick cabinet or box*). DS *of the bed, two chairs. In one sits Nanny Ogg, reading a paper; in the other sits Granny Weatherwax, reading "'The Joye of Snacks"*

Nanny Ogg I really don't think we needed to shove the other bed up against the door, Esme.
Granny Weatherwax You can't be too careful. Supposing some man started rattling the knob in the middle of the night?
Nanny Ogg (*sadly*) Not at our time of life.

We hear splashing, off, as of water being poured into a bath

Granny Weatherwax Gytha Ogg! You are the most ...

The pouring ends with a trickle and a couple of splashes

Someone filling a bath?
Nanny Ogg Yes. I suppose it could be someone filling a bath.

More splashing noises

Granny Weatherwax Yes. A man getting into a bath.

Nanny gets up and crosses to the wall

Where are you going, Gytha?
Nanny Ogg Seein' if there's a knot-hole in this wood somewhere. Ah. Here's one ...
Granny Weatherwax Come back here!
Nanny Ogg Sorry, Esme.

Singing can now be heard off stage; Enrico Basilica's pleasant tenor voice, with a "bathroom echo"

Enrico Basilica (*singing; off*) Show me the way to go home, I'm tired and I want to go to bed ...
Nanny Ogg Someone's enjoying themselves, anyway.

There is a knock at the offstage door

Voice (*calling; off*) Mr Basilica?

Enrico Basilica (*continuing the song in Italian; off*) ... *per via terra, mare o schiuma* ... (*Speaking*) Come in-a!

Voice (*off*) I've brought you your hot-water bottle, sir.

Enrico Basilica (*off*) Thank you verr' mucha. (*Singing*) *Indicatame la strada* ... to go home ... (*Speaking*) Good-eeeeevening, friends!

Granny Weatherwax Well, well, well. It seems that our Mr Slugg is a secret polyglot.

Nanny Ogg Fancy! And you haven't even looked through the knot-hole!

Granny Weatherwax Gytha, is there anything in this world that you can't make sound grubby?

Nanny Ogg Haven't found it yet!

Granny Weatherwax What I meant was that when he mutters in his sleep or sings in his bath he talks just like you and me. But when he thinks people are listening, he comes over all foreign-like. I reckon that our Mr Slugg may be very close to that Enrico Basilica — in fact, I reckon they're ——

There is a scuffling from the cat box, and some anguished yowling

Gytha! I hope it's not happening again!

Nanny Ogg It can't be!

Granny Weatherwax You told me it only happened when he was cornered!

Nanny Ogg I don't understand it!

Granny Weatherwax Hold on, though — he's a cat at the moment Gytha, he's only wearing a cat collar! You'd just better magic up some clothes p.d.q.! Come on, concentrate, woman!

Nanny Ogg Oh, Esme ... !

Granny Weatherwax Do it, Gytha!

Nanny Ogg Yes, Esme!

The two witches focus on the cat box, which continues to rattle away, with the cat noises sounding increasingly human. Lighting and sound effects. Strobe?

> *Greebo emerges, rising out of the ground with the cat box on his head. He is dressed in a sort of New Romantic outfit: full-sleeved shirt, black leather waistcoat, black trousers and thigh-boots. He sports a patch over one eye. When he is fully upright, Greebo removes the cat box from his head*

Granny Weatherwax Well, well, well. Hallo again, Greebo!

Nanny Ogg (*tickling Greebo under the chin*) Ooza ickle-wickle, then?

Black-out

Scene 9
On Board The Coach

Granny and Nanny sit on one side, Enrico Basilica and his Manager on the other

Nanny Ogg Well, here we are again then. (*Pause*) That was some good singing last night.

Manager I'm afraid Señor Basilica doesn't speak Morporkian, ma'am. But I will translate for you, if you like.

Nanny Ogg What? Then how come — ow!

Granny Weatherwax Sorry. Elbow must've slipped.

Nanny Ogg I was saying that he was — ow!

Granny Weatherwax Dear me, seem to have done it again. This gentleman is just telling us that his friend doesn't speak our language, Gytha.

Nanny Ogg Eh? But ... What? Oh. But ... Ah. Really? Oh. All right. Oh yes, eats our pies, though, when — ow!

Granny Weatherwax 'Scuse my friend. It's her time of life. She gets confused. We did enjoy his singing. We heard him through the wall.

Manager You are most fortunate. Some people have to wait for years to hear Señor Basilica ...

Nanny Ogg Prob'ly waiting for him to finish his dinner...

Manager In fact, in Genua last month Señor Basilica made ten thousand people shed tears.

Nanny Ogg Hah, I can do that. I don't see how there's anything special ——

Manager Señor Basilica's fame has spread far and wide ...

Nanny Ogg A bit like Señor Basilica himself, then ...

Granny Weatherwax Well, well. It's nice and warm in Genua. I expect Señor Basilica misses his home. And what do you do, young sir?

Manager I am his translator and his manager. Er, you have the advantage of me, ma'am.

Granny Weatherwax Yes, indeed. (*Pause*) Well, it must be very tiring, chasing around after a big opera star. In fact, I expect you could do with a short sleep right now!

The Manager falls instantly asleep

Well, now there's just you and me, Gytha. And Señor Basilica of course, who doesn't speak our language.

Enrico Basilica Ladies! Dear ladies! I beg you, for pity's sake...

Nanny Ogg Have you done anything bad, Mr Henry Slugg?

Enrico Basilica No.

Granny Weatherwax He's tellin' the truth. You don't want people to know where you're really from, do you? People only value things if they comes from a long way away. Where are you really from, Henry Slugg?

Enrico Basilica I grew up in Rookery Yard in Ankh-Morpork's Shades. It was a rough place. There were only three ways out. You could sing your way out or fight your way out.

Nanny Ogg What was the third way?

Enrico Basilica Oh, you could go down that little alleyway into Shamlegger Street and then cut down into Treacle Mine Road. But no-one amounted to anything who went that way. I made a few coppers singing in taverns and so on, but when I tried for anything better they said, "What's your name?" and I said Henry Slugg and they'd laugh. I needed to change my name, but people knew me in Ankh-Morpork so I moved to Genua. Then, when I was famous ...

Granny Weatherwax You were stuck in Enrico Basilica.

Enrico Basilica The worst thing is that everywhere I go they go to special efforts to cook me pasta. In tomato sauce! With boiled squid! They think I'll enjoy it, but all I really want is a plate of roast mutton with clootie dumplings.

Nanny Ogg Why don't you say?

Enrico Basilica Enrico Basilica eats pasta. There's not much I can do about it now. Here, (*he draws out two opera tickets*) please accept these as a token of my thanks for the pork pie.

Granny Weatherwax Why thank you. We shall be sure to go.

Enrico Basilica And now, if you will excuse me. I must catch up on my sleep.

Granny Weatherwax Don't worry, I shouldn't think it's had time to get far away.

Enrico falls asleep

Nanny Ogg He's well away.

Granny Weatherwax Yes, and I might say how relieved I am that Greebo is back in his proper shape this morning!

Nanny Ogg Yes, Esme. Here, you want to visit the opera?

Granny Weatherwax I don't like fiction. As you know. Trouble is, it has its own force of attraction. It's where reality meets fantasy. Witches is drawn to places where two states collide. We feel the pull of doorways, boundaries, mirrors, masks ——

Nanny Ogg —— and stages.

Black-out

Scene 10
The Opera House. Backstage

Some chorus on stage, chatting and so on. In one corner of the stage is propped a broom. Occasionally a stagehand crosses with a pot of paint/bit of scenery or whatever. Agnes Nitt is chatting to one of the chorus

Christine enters

The chorus people drift off during the following

Christine Perdita! Hallo! do you like my new dress? Isn't it fetching?
Agnes Nitt Yes. Very fetching.
Christine And I have a secret admirer! Isn't that thrilling? All great singers have them!
Agnes Nitt A secret admirer?
Christine Yes! This dress! It arrived at the stage door just now! (*A new thought*) I say, you look a bit tired ... Oh, we swapped rooms, didn't we? I was so silly! D'you know, I could have sworn I heard someone singing in the night — scales and things?
Agnes Nitt You know that's funny, because I was right next door to you and I didn't hear a thing.
Christine Oh? Well, that's all right then! Are you going in to breakfast?
Agnes Nitt Er, yes. Come on.

Christine and Agnes Nitt exit

For a second or two, the stage is empty

Mrs Plinge enters

Mrs Plinge Walter! Walter? (*She crosses to the onstage broom*) Hm. Now where are you, Walter? It's not like you to miss a part of your routine, my lad. I'd better make a start for the lad, or he'll get himself in trouble. (*She starts to sweep*)

We hear Mr Pounder whistling a tune off stage

Who is that?

Mr Pounder enters along the balcony

Mr Pounder? You should know better! It's terrible bad luck to whistle on stage.
Mr Pounder Bad luck? I'm whistling 'cos of good luck, see.
Mrs Plinge And it's bad luck to keep talking about the Ghost, Mr Pounder. He doesn't like it, you know.
Mr Pounder If you knew what I know, you'd be a happy man, too. O'course, in your case you'd be a happy woman, on account of you being a woman. Ah, some of the things I've seen, Mrs Plinge.

Mrs Plinge Found gold on your travels round the theatre, Mr Pounder?

Mr Pounder heads for the exit

Mr Pounder (*as he exits*) Could be. Could be gold, Mrs Plinge.

He leaves. There is the thump of sandbags hitting the floor, off

Mrs Plinge Pardon, Mr Pounder? Mr Pounder? Are you there? Mr Pounder? Coo-eee? Hallo?

Pounder's hat falls from the roof on to the stage. Mrs Plinge looks up. Pounder's legs appear, dangling below a masking cloth in the balcony

Mr Pounder?

Black-out

Mrs Plinge exits

The Lights come back up straightaway on the balcony alone. Pounder is there, looking up at "his" legs

Mr Pounder Hey, who's that? Oh. It's me, I suppose.

The Death of Rats appears at the balcony rail. He is a rat's skeleton (slightly larger than life), wearing black robes and carrying a small scythe

Death of Rats SQUEAK.
Mr Pounder Er, I'm dead, aren't I ... ?
Death of Rats SQUEAK.
Mr Pounder I spent all me life as a ratcatcher. Um. Is that why it's you that's come for me instead of the tall bloke with the scythe?
Death of Rats SQUEAK.
Mr Pounder (*who is beginning to show signs of "rattishness"*) I always heard that rats had a Death of their own. I heard he was called the Grim Squeaker.

The Death of Rats turns and looks at the audience

Look, it was just a job, OK? Nuffin' personal like, see? (*He suddenly "shrinks" about a foot*) Here. what's happening to me?
Death of Rats SQUEAK.

Mr Pounder Reincarnated? What as? Oh no! No, no! But I don't believe in reincarnation!

Death of Rats SQUEAK.

Mr Pounder What do you mean: reincarnation believes in me? (*He suddenly shrinks from view*) No-o-o-o-o!!! (*Brief pause. We hear his voice, out of vision*) Squeak!

Black-out

Scene 11
On Stage

A small crowd are staring up at Pounder's feet. Mrs Plinge holds out Pounder's hat to Mr Bucket. Salzella is also on stage

Bucket bursts in, waving a letter

Seldom Bucket Mr Salzella! Mr Salzella!! (*He follows everyone's eyes and sees the "body"*) Oh gods. He's struck again, hasn't he?

Mrs Plinge It just fell out of the flies! His poor hat!

Seldom Bucket (*looking up*) Oh dear. And I thought he'd written such a polite letter ... (*He hands the letter to Salzella*)

The text appears on the screen:
   "I will be obliged if Christine sings the role of Iodine in 'La Triviata' tonight. The weather continues fine. I trust you are well.
   Yrs,
   The Opera Ghost."

Salzella (*producing a letter*) Really? Then read this one. It's addressed to you as well.

Bucket opens the letter. The second letter appears on the screen:
   "Hahahaha! Ahahahaha!
   Yrs,
   The Opera Ghost
   PS Ahahahahaha!!!!!"

Seldom Bucket Who's the poor fellow up there?

Salzella Mr Pounder, the ratcatcher. Rope dropped round his neck. Other end attached to some sandbags. They went down. He went — up.

Seldom Bucket I don't understand! Is this man mad?

Salzella Well now. A man who wears evening dress all the time, lurks in the shadows and occasionally kills people. Then he sends little notes, writing maniacal laughter. Five exclamation marks again, I see. We have to ask ourselves: is this the career of a sane man?

Seldom Bucket But why is he doing it?

Salzella That is only a relevant question if he is sane. He may be doing it because the little yellow pixies tell him to.

Seldom Bucket Sane? How could he be sane? The atmosphere in this place would drive anyone crazy. I may be the only one around here with my feet on the ground! You lot! Haven't you any work to do? Sets to build? Dances to rehearse? And don't stand around on both feet! Jump up and down! On one leg!

Everyone hops off except Salzella and Seldom Bucket

What was I saying?

Salzella You were saying that you have both feet on the ground. Unlike the corps de ballet. And the corpse de Mr Pounder.

Seldom Bucket I think that comment is in rather poor taste. What should we do ...?

Salzella We ought to close down; search the place from ——

Seldom Bucket Close down ...? We can't afford to close down! We seem to make thousands a week but we spend thousands a week, too! I don't know where it goes. I thought running this place was just a matter of getting bums on seats, but every time I look up I see a bum swinging in the air. (*His gaze moves around, at roof level, from Pounder's feet to the chandelier*) What's he going to do next —— oh no! He wouldn't, would he? That would shut us down!

Salzella Look, it weighs more than a ton. The supporting rope is stout and true. The winch is padlocked when it's not in use. It's safe.

Bucket looks unconvinced

I'll have a man guard it every minute there's a performance. I'll do it personally, if you like.

Seldom Bucket And he wants Christine to sing tonight. She's got a voice like a whistle!

Salzella That at least, is not a problem.

Seldom Bucket Isn't it? It's a key role!

Salzella Ah, now let me explain something else to you about opera. From time to time in opera a major star will be too ill to perform. Laryngitis, perhaps, or a little too much scumble in the bar between shows. You know; they can still walk, but the singing could be a problem? Well, when that happens, we get one of the chorus who can sing the role to stand behind them on stage and, well, sing the part for them.

Seldom Bucket Really?

Salzella Really. Now, let's go and talk to young Perdita Nitt, mmm?

They exit

Black-out

SCENE 12
The Publishers

Outside the publishers. Granny and Nanny knock at the door

Nanny Ogg Esme. Why did we have to come here straightway? I'd have preferred to unpack and get something to eat, first.

Granny Weatherwax 'Cos you've been swindled out of your life savings.

Nanny Ogg Three dollars?

Granny Weatherwax Well, it's all you've actually saved. You've been exploited.

> *Goatberger walks up to them. He is carrying a large cut-out display board. Although we only ever see its back (on which is written "Joye of Snackes Display Stand"), it is clearly the cutout of a nude female*

Goatberger Ladies? Are you trying to gain entry to my publishing house?

Granny Weatherwax We've come about this book.

Nanny Ogg I'm Mrs Ogg.

Goatberger Oh yes? Can you identify yourself?

Nanny Ogg (*rootling in her capacious handbag as if looking for an ID card; then drawing out a mirror and examining herself in it*) Yes, that's me all right.

Goatberger Hah! Well, I happen to know what Gytha Ogg looks like. And she does not look like you.

Granny Weatherwax And how would you know what Gytha Ogg looks like?

Goatberger Because she sent me her picture. See? We used it on the point-of-sale display material. (*He shows the panel to Granny Weatherwax*)

Granny Weatherwax (*looking at the panel, then turning and glaring at Nanny Ogg*) Oh yes. That's Gytha Ogg all right. I remember when that artist came up to Lancre for the summer.

Nanny Ogg I wore my hair longer in those days.

Granny Weatherwax Just as well. (*To Goatberger*) That's Gytha Ogg all right. Except it's out by about sixty years and several layers of clothing. This is Gytha Ogg. Right here.

Goatberger You're telling me this came up with "Bananana Soup Surprise"?

Nanny Ogg Did you try it?

Goatberger Mr Cropper the head printer did, yes.

Granny Weatherwax Was he surprised?

Goatberger Not one half as surprised as Mrs Cropper!

Nanny Ogg It can take people like that. I think perhaps I overdo the nutmeg.

Granny Weatherwax But right now she'd like some more money. She'd like a little bit of money for every book you've sold.

Nanny Ogg I don't expect to be treated like royalty.

Goatberger And what if I refuse?

Nanny Ogg I really don't think you'd like exploring that option.

Goatberger Of course, things are very difficult at the moment. People just aren't buying books ...

Granny Weatherwax Everyone I knows buys your almanack. I reckon everyone in Lancre buys your almanack. Heck, everyone in the Ramtops buys your almanack — including the dwarfs. That's a lot of half-dollars. And Gytha's book seems to be doing very well.

Goatberger Well, of course, I'm glad it's going so well, but what with distribution, paying the pedlars, wear and tear on ——

Granny Weatherwax Your almanack will last a household all winter, with care. Providing no-one's ill.

Nanny Ogg My Jason buys two copies. Course, he's got a big family.

Granny Weatherwax stares at Goatberger during the following

Goatberger Yes, but of course I don't actually have to pay you anything. You paid me to print it, and I gave you your money back. In fact I think our accounts department made a slight error in your favour, but I won't ... (*He falters under Granny Weatherwax's stare*)

Granny Weatherwax Your Almanack's full of useful predictions for the coming year. Handy stuff, predicting. I can't do that clever stuff that you do, mind — you know, looking years ahead. But I'm pretty damn accurate over the next thirty seconds.

Goatberger Indeed? And what's going to happen in thirty seconds?

Granny Weatherwax leans forward and whispers in Goatberger's ear

Oh. Um. Er, ladies — please — come into my offices. I'm sure we can reach an amicable arrangement.

They exit

Black-out

SCENE 13
The Opera House. On Stage

This is played, "Joyce Grenfell style", with Dr Underschaft and André (sitting at the "harmonium") on stage, addressing Agnes Nitt who is in the "fourth wall". All her lines are delivered into the microphone backstage, so that they come from the auditorium speakers

Dr Underschaft Right. Now then. Good-morning, Perdita, how are you?
Agnes Nitt (*over speakers*) Fine. Thank you, Dr Underschaft.
Dr Underschaft Now then, we will start with the famous "Departure" aria. It is quite a little masterpiece. Not one of the great operatic highlights, you understand, but very memorable nevertheless. "*Questa maledetta*", sings Iodine, as she tells Peccadillo how hard it is for her to leave him ... (*He sings. The words can be made to fit Mozart's aria: "Voi Che Sapete"*) "*Questa maledetta porta si blocca, Si blocca comunque diavolo lo faccio..!*" (*He stops and dabs at his eye with his hanky*) When Gigli sang it, there wasn't a dry eye in the house. I was there. It was then that I decided that ... Oh, great days. Now then. You have your score? Right, then let us run through it. André?

The introduction plays, but when the singing starts it is Dr Underschaft's voice that we hear over the speakers. André stops playing. He is laughing. The singing stops too

Ahem!
Agnes Nitt Was I doing something wrong?
Dr Underschaft You were singing tenor.
André She was singing in your voice, Doctor.
Dr Underschaft Aah. right. Well perhaps you could sing it as Christine would sing it, hmm?

The introduction plays, and when the singing starts, it is indeed Christine's reedy voice that we hear. André is again amused. Dr Underschaft is nonplussed

Yes, yes. Accurately observed. I daresay you're right. But could we start again and, er, perhaps you would sing it how you think it ought to be sung?

This time it is Agnes Nitt's voice that we hear, singing the aria splendidly

Dr Underschaft seems overcome with emotion. Clasping his hanky to his mouth, he rushes for the exit

I'm sorry! Will you please excuse me.

He exits

Agnes Nitt now walks on to the stage from the back of the auditorium

Agnes Nitt Er ... was that all right?

André I think you just reawakened Dr Underschaft's memories of the Great Gigli. That was astounding.

Agnes Nitt Thank you. But I still don't understand the words. What did it all mean?

André Oh. Um. well, roughly it means: "This damn door sticks, this damn door sticks. It sticks no matter what the hell I do. It's marked 'Pull' and indeed I am pulling. Perhaps it should be marked 'Push'?"

Agnes Nitt That's it? But I thought it was supposed to be romantic?

André It is. This is opera, not real life. The words don't matter. It's the feeling that matters. Look, I'll have to go ... Er, look, I'm sorry if I frightened you last night.

Agnes Nitt Oh. It's all right. I wasn't frightened.

André Er — you didn't mention it to anyone, did you? I'd hate people to think I was worrying over nothing.

Agnes Nitt I hadn't given it another thought, to tell you the truth. I know you can't be the Ghost, if that's what's worrying you.

André Me? The Ghost? Ha, ha, ha!

Agnes joins in with the laughter

So ... er ... see you tomorrow, then.

Agnes Nitt Fine.

André leaves

Christine enters

Christine Oh, Agnes! Have you heard? I'm to sing the part of Iodine tonight! Isn't that wonderful? (*She rushes up to Agnes Nitt and hugs her*) And I've heard they're already letting you into the chorus!

Agnes Nitt Er, yes.

Christine Because my father told me that one day a little pixie would arrive to help me achieve my great ambition, and, do you know, I think that little pixie is you! Oh, by the way, I thought we'd swap rooms back again! I'll need that big mirror now that I'm to be a prima donna! You don't mind, do you?!

Agnes Nitt What? Oh, no. No, of course not. If you're sure. Come on, then, let's go and swap our stuff back, mm?

They exit

There is a brief pause

Dr Underschaft enters, from a different direction

Dr Underschaft Right, now. Sorry, my dear. I don't know what came over me. Hrm. Now ... Oh. Oh well. Dear me, what a voice she has. Now why on earth won't they let her play the role? I know she's a little — robust, but then the Great Gigli once crushed a tenor to death and no-one thought any the worse of her for it. It's the voice that's important. (*He starts to move the "harmonium" back into the wings. As he gets there, he sees someone in the wings*) Hallo? What are you doing in there?

The Phantom (Salzella) steps out, still pulling a mask over his face (which is nevertheless obscured from the audience by his hand)

Oh my gods! Aha! You're the Opera Ghost! Now I've got you!

The Phantom puts his hands around Underschaft's neck

Aargh!

The Phantom drags Dr Underschaft off into the wings leaving Dr Underschaft's glasses behind on stage

A couple of the Opera's stage crew, Kevin and Hron, appear

Kevin Look at that, Hron! Blimmin' typical, innit. They've only gone and left the harmonium right in the middle of the stage. Just expect us to move it for 'em, I 'spose.
Hron Yus. And not even a please or a thank you for doin' it, Kevin. Blimmin' typical.
Kevin If I 'ad 'im 'ere, Hron, I'd give that Dr Underschaft a good shaking by the froat. Typical. Come on, then.

They start to lug the harmonium off. As they near the entrance ——

Granny Weatherwax and Nanny Ogg enter. Nanny Ogg has Greebo (the cat) curled around her neck. She is walking a trifle bowleggedly; there is a chinking sound from her drawers

There is a bit of jiggling so that the two couples can get past each other

Nanny Ogg That's a very small organ, young man.

Off stage we hear a voice running up a scale (La, la, la ...); this continues during the following

How much did we get again?

Granny Weatherwax Three thousand, two hundred and seventy dollars and eighty-seven pence.

Nanny Ogg I thought it was nice of him to look in all the ashtrays for all the old copper he could round up. How much was that again?

Granny Weatherwax Three thousand, two hundred and seventy dollars and eighty-seven pence.

Nanny Ogg I never had seventy dollars before.

Granny Weatherwax I didn't say seventy, I said ——

Nanny Ogg I know, I know. But I'm working my way up to it, gradual-like. I'll say this about money. It certainly chafes.

Granny Weatherwax I don't know why you have to keep your purse in your knicker leg.

Nanny Ogg It's the last place anyone would look. You're going to have to be polite to me, now I'm rich.

Granny Weatherwax Yes indeed. Don't think I'm not considering that.

Nanny Ogg I don't think we're supposed to be in this bit, Esme. I think the audience usually ——

Granny Weatherwax We're witches, Gytha. We go where we damn well like. Someone's singing. Listen.

The voice sings "Doh, Re, Mi, Fah, Soh, La, Ti, Doh!"

That's opera, right enough. Sounds foreign to me.

Nanny Ogg Er. Could be. There's always a lot going on, I know that. Our Nev said that sometimes they do different operations every night.

Granny Weatherwax How did he find that out?

Nanny Ogg (*looking up*) Well, there was a lot of lead, and it took him a while to shift all of it. He said he liked the noisy ones. 'Cos he could hum along. And 'cos no-one could hear him hammering.

Granny Weatherwax Did you notice young Agnes nearly bump into us back there? Completely ignored us. Luckily.

Nanny Ogg Yes, it was all I could do not to wave.

Granny Weatherwax She wasn't very pleased to see us, was she?

Nanny Ogg No. Suspicious, that. I mean, she sees two friendly faces from back home ... Hey, remember those eyes in the teacup back home? She could be under the gaze of some strange occult force. Remember Mr Scruple?

Granny Weatherwax That wasn't a strange occult force. That was wind.
Nanny Ogg Well, it certainly seemed strangely occult for a while. Especially if the windows were shut.

Walter Plinge enters, carrying some posters and a paste pot

Walter Plinge Oh, er, oh. Um, excuse me — ladies. Er, the show must go on, you know.

Nanny Ogg and Granny Weatherwax step aside

Thank you. (*He heads across the stage*)
Granny Weatherwax What's your name, young man?
Walter Plinge Walter!
Granny Weatherwax That's a nice beret you have there.
Walter Plinge My mum made it for me!

Walter Plinge exits

Nanny Ogg You know, I wouldn't mind seein' an operation. Señor Basilica did give us the tickets.
Granny Weatherwax Oh, you know me. I can't be having with that sort of thing. (*Meaning: Of course I want to, but you've got to persuade me*)
Nanny Ogg I expect it's having ideas above our station. I expect if we went in they'd say, "Be off, you nasty ole crones ... "
Granny Weatherwax Oh they would, would they?
Nanny Ogg I don't expect they want common folk like what we are comin' in with all those smart nobby people.
Granny Weatherwax Is that a fact? Is that a fact, madam?

Kevin and Hron enter

Nasty old crones, eh?
Kevin I'm sorry?
Granny Weatherwax So I would think! Now look, it says here we've got tickets for — it says here the stalls. Stalls? I'm not sittin' in with the damn' horses. Where does everyone else sit?
Kevin Well, there's the Circle, the Grand Tier, um, the Gods....
Granny Weatherwax The Gods! That sounds more like it. We'll exchange our tickets.
Kevin You want to swap Stalls tickets for Gods tickets?
Granny Weatherwax Yes. And don't ask us for any more money. Hah!
Kevin Er, no. I don't think they'd ask you for more money. But you'll have to hurry; the performance will be starting shortly.

Hron Er, excuse me, madam, but what's that on your shoulders?
Nanny Ogg It's — a fur collar.
Hron But I just saw its tail move.
Nanny Ogg Yes, I happen to believe in beauty without cruelty.

Nanny Ogg and Granny Weatherwax sweep out

Seldom Bucket (*off*) Dr Underschaft! Dr Underschaft?

Seldom Bucket enters with Salzella

Salzella Ah. You men. Have you seen Dr Underschaft?
Hron No, Mr Salzella. There was just the harmonium here when we come
to clear up after 'is rehearsal.
Salzella Thank you. Don't let us keep you from your proper duties.

Kevin and Hron exit

Where is he? We can't search the entire building! The place is a maze. (*He
sees Dr Underschaft's glasses*) Hallo. What have we here?
Seldom Bucket He might have just wandered off somewhere, I suppose.
Salzella Not without these. He's blind as a bat otherwise.
Seldom Bucket But we can't be certain that something's happened to him.
Salzella Oh yes? You didn't say that when we opened that double-bass case.
You were certain he was going to be inside it. Admit it.
Seldom Bucket I — wasn't expecting to see just a smashed double-bass, I
admit. But I was feeling a bit flustered. (*He checks his watch*) It's almost
curtain-up. We'd better take our places. (*He glances up at the chandelier*)
Salzella Don't worry, Bucket. It's as safe as houses.

Salzella and Seldom Bucket exit

The Lights cross-fade to the balcony

Scene 14
In The Gods

*Played in the balcony. There are two rows of four chairs visible. All but the
two at the stage left of the front row are occupied. Granny Weatherwax and
Nanny Ogg enter and make their way in front of the occupants of the other
two front row seats. Nanny Ogg sits next to the Woman With Chocs; Granny
Weatherwax sits in front of the Man With Glasses and the Man With a Death
Wish*

Nanny Ogg 'Scuse me. 'Scuse me. Was that your foot?

They sit. The Lights in the Gods dim, and the scene is lit by lights from the "stage". We hear some distant music. The two witches sit silent for a moment or two. Behind them, the Man With a Death Wish tries to peer around them

Granny Weatherwax What's happening now?
Nanny Ogg Er... (*To the person next to her*) 'Scuse me, could I borrow your programme?

The Woman With Chocs hands Nanny Ogg the programme

Thank you. (*To the Man With Glasses behind her*) 'Scuse me, could I borrow your spectacles?

The man hands over his spectacles

So kind. Now then ... (*Pause. She consults the programme*) This is the Overture. It's a kind of free sample of what's goin' to happen. S'got a summary of the story here, too. "La Triviata." (*She pauses*) Well, it's quite simple, really. A lot of people are in love with one another, there's considerable dressing up as other people and general confusion. There's a cheeky servant, chorus of gypsies. Your basic opera, reely.
Woman With Chocs Shhh!
Granny Weatherwax Wish we'd brought something to eat.
Nanny Ogg I think I've got some peppermints in me knicker leg. (*She produces some peppermints and eats one during the following*)
Woman With Chocs Shh!
Man With Glasses Erm, could I have my spectacles back, please?
Nanny Ogg 'Ere you go. Not very good, are they?

Nanny Ogg hands the spectacles back

Woman With Chocs Madam, your fur stole is eating my chocolates!
Man With Death Wish (*to Granny Weatherwax*) Madam, kindly remove your hat.

Nanny Ogg chokes on her peppermint

Granny Weatherwax (*turning slowly to face the Man With a Death Wish*) You do know what a woman in a pointy hat is, don't you?
Man With Death Wish Yes, madam. A woman in a pointy hat is sitting in front of me.

There is a pause

Granny Weatherwax I do beg your pardon. I can see I was inadvertently
bad-mannered. Pray excuse me. (*She takes off her hat*)
Nanny Ogg You feeling all right, Esme?
Granny Weatherwax Never better.
Woman With Chocs I assure you, madam. Your fur IS eating my chocolates.
And it's started on the second layer!
Nanny Ogg Oh dear. Show him the little map on the lid, will you? He's only
after the truffles and you can soon wipe the dribble off the others.
Man With Glasses Do you mind being quiet?
Nanny Ogg I don't mind. It's this lady and her chocolates that's making all
the noise ...

There is a momentary lull

Here, it says here that Dame Timpani, who sings the part of Quizella, is a
diva. (*She pronounces it "diver"*) This must be her part-time job, I s'pose.
Good idea on account of you have to be able to hold your breath. Good
trainin' for the singing ... There's Agnes! Hey, that's Agnes!
Granny Weatherwax Stop waving and sit down. What's Agnes singing?
Nanny Ogg Oh no, it's not her singing — it's (*she consults the programme*)
some girl called Christine.
Granny Weatherwax It's Agnes. Close your eyes and listen, you daft old
baggage.
Nanny Ogg It's Agnes! But the other girl's moving her lips. That's not right,
stealing our Agnes' voice.
Granny Weatherwax Gytha, tell me if those curtains down there in that
private box just moved.
Nanny Ogg I just saw them twitch, Esme.
Granny Weatherwax There's fear here, Gytha. I can feel it in the very fabric
of the building. (*She leaps to her feet*) NO!
Nanny Ogg Esme — sit down.
Granny Weatherwax (*sitting*) This is a bad one, Gytha. It's all twisted up.
I ain't so sure that I can make it happen right. The poor soul ... (*She snaps
out of this mood*) Come on, Gytha.
Nanny Ogg What? Where?
Granny Weatherwax To see what's behind those curtains.

*Granny Weatherwax and Nanny Ogg make their way out again, leaving
Greebo behind*

Nanny Ogg 'Scuse me. 'Scuse me.

Granny Weatherwax and Nanny Ogg exit. We hear the following lines of dialogue over the speakers

Nanny Ogg (*voice-over*) Gytha, I was glad to see you didn't lose your temper with that man about your hat.

Granny Weatherwax (*voice-over*) No point. He's going to be dead tomorrow. Run over by a cart, I think.

Nanny Ogg (*voice-over*) Why didn't you tell him?

Granny Weatherwax (*voice-over*) I could be wrong.

Nanny Ogg (*voice-over*) Oh bugger!

Granny Weatherwax (*voice-over*) What?

Nanny Ogg (*voice-over*) I left Greebo up there!

Granny Weatherwax (*voice-over*) Well, he likes meeting new people. Good grief, this place is a maze!

The Lights change; the scene is now the corridor behind the opera boxes. The music is quieter here

Granny Weatherwax and Nanny Ogg enter

Granny Weatherwax Ah, this is it. The corridor behind those private boxes. (*She makes to try one of the "doors"*)

Mrs Plinge enters carrying a tray of drinks

Mrs Plinge Can I help you ladies?

Granny Weatherwax We were just wondering, which person in these boxes likes to sit with the curtains nearly shut?

Mrs Plinge's hands begin to shake, rattling the tray

Nanny Ogg Here, shall I hold that for you? We wouldn't want you spilling all them nice drinks.

Mrs Plinge What do you know about Box Eight?

Granny Weatherwax Ah. Box Eight. That's be the one, yes. That's this one over here, isn't it?

Mrs Plinge No, please — it'll bring terrible bad luck.

Granny Weatherwax Stand aside, please, madam, or ...

Nanny Ogg Or what?

Granny Weatherwax No. No, I reckon we'll leave it for now.

Mrs Plinge (*crying*) I don't know what's happening. It never used to be like this ...

Nanny Ogg Here. (*She proffers a grubby hanky*) Have a good blow.

Mrs Plinge There was none of this killing people ... He just wanted somewhere to watch the opera — it made him feel better...

Granny Weatherwax Who's this we're talkin' about?

Nanny Ogg gives Granny Weatherwax a warning look. The music fades to silence

Mrs Plinge He'd unlock it for an hour every Friday for me to tidy up and there was always a little note saying thank you or apologizing for the peanuts down the seat — and where was the harm in it, I'd like to know. And now there's people dropping like flies from the flies. They say it's him, but I know he never meant any harm ...

Nanny Ogg Course not. What's your name, dear?

Mrs Plinge Mrs Plinge.

Granny Weatherwax I think it would be a good idea if we was to take you home, Mrs Plinge.

Mrs Plinge Oh dear! I've got all these ladies and gentlemen to see to! And anyway, it's dangerous going home this time of night ... Walter walks me home, but he's got to stay late tonight ...

Granny Weatherwax Dangerous, eh? Well, we can't see you upset like this. I'll walk you home, and Mrs Ogg here will see to things here.

Mrs Plinge Only I've got to attend to the boxes; I've got all these drinks to serve.

Nanny Ogg Don't you worry, there's nothing I don't know about drinks.

Mrs Plinge And what about our Walter? He'll worry himself silly ...

Granny Weatherwax Walter's your son? Wears a beret?

Mrs Plinge Only I always come back for him if he's working late ...

Granny Weatherwax You come back for him — but he sees you home?

Mrs Plinge It's ... He's ... He's ... He's a good boy.

Granny Weatherwax I'm sure he is, Mrs Plinge. (*To Nanny Ogg*) I'll be back as soon as I can.

Mrs Plinge and Granny Weatherwax exit

Nanny starts to drink the contents of the tray. Bells can be heard ringing in the various boxes. They slowly fade

Voice (*off*) Where are those drinks, woman?

Nanny Ogg (*to the audience*) Well, they seem to want their drinks. I expect you'll be wanting yours. Be back here in fifteen minutes, though, please.

Black-out

ACT II

On Stage

In the dark, there is a scream

The Lights come up

Chaos greets us. People mill around. On stage is the body of Dr Underschaft with a sheet beside it. Nanny Ogg saunters on

Nanny Ogg Evenin'. What's goin' on? Excuse me, let me through, I'm a nosy person. (*She elbows her way through the throng around the body*) Oh dear. Poor man. What happened?

Kevin When we let the backdrop go up at the end of the scene, Dr Underschaft came down. He'd been attached to the counterweight! Mr Bucket says he must have got caught up in the ——

Colette He didn't get caught in anything! It was the Ghost! He could still be up there!

Giselle Mr Salzella's sent some stage hands up there to flush him out!

Nanny Ogg Have they got flaming torches? Got to have flaming torches when you're tracking down evil monsters. Well-known fact.

Kevin That's true.

Colette She's right, you know.

Nanny Ogg Well-known fact, dear. Did they have flaming torches?

Kevin Don't think so. Just ordinary lanterns.

Nanny Ogg Oh, that's no good. That's for smugglers, lanterns. For evil monsters ...

Arno Excuse me, boys and girls. Now, I'm sure you're all familiar with the phrase, "the show must go on".

There are groans

Now, we don't actually know what happened ——

Giselle Really? Shall we guess?

Arno —— but we have men up in the fly loft now, and Mr Bucket has authorized me to say that there will be an additional two dollars bonus in recognition of your bravely agreeing to continue with the show ...

Hron Money? After a shock like this? Money? He thinks he can offer us a couple of dollars and we'll agree to stay on this cursed stage!

Colette Shame!

Giselle Heartless!

Kevin Unthinkable!

Solange Should be at least four!

Crowd Right! Right!

Arno For shame, my friends! To talk about a few dollars when a dead man is lying there. Have you no respect for his memory?

Solange He's right. (*Pause*) A few dollars is disrespectful. Five dollars or nothing!

Arno Five dollars?

There is general agreement

Right. Come on, then. The show must go on.

Everyone drifts off except Dr Underschaft, Walter Plinge and Nanny Ogg

Nanny Ogg picks up the sheet next to the body

Nanny Ogg Can you give me a hand with this, mister?

Walter Plinge He won't wake up!

Nanny Ogg That's right, love. You're Walter, ain't you?

Walter Plinge He was always good to me and my mum! He never give me a kick! Miss, they say it was the Ghost, miss! It weren't the Ghost, miss! My mum'd know what to do!

Nanny Ogg Yes ... Well, she's gone home early, Walter.

Walter Plinge She mustn't walk home without Walter to look after her! 's dangerous!

Nanny Ogg That's right, dear. But I need you to put poor Dr Underschaft somewhere safe until after the show. Understand? And I'm Mrs Ogg.

Walter Plinge gawps at her, then nods sharply

Good boy.

Bernard, a stage hand, enters, heading across the stage. As he passes Nanny Ogg, she grabs his arm in a grip of iron

Walter Plinge exits during the following dialogue

(*To Bernard*) Hallo, dearie. But d'you know anyone round here called Agnes? Agnes Nitt?

Bernard You mean Perdita Nitt? I think she's seeing to Christine. In Mr Salzella's office.

Nanny Ogg Christine. She's the tall thin girl in white?

Bernard That's right.

Nanny Ogg And I expect you're going to tell me where this office is?

Bernard Er, am I ... er, yes. It's just along the stage there. First door on the right.

Nanny Ogg What a good boy to help an old lady. And wouldn't be a good idea if you helped young Walter here to move Dr Underschaft?

Bernard (*noting Walter's absence*) Um ... ?

Nanny Ogg Ah. I expect he was a bit upset. Only to be expected. Well, a strapping lad like you can probably manage on his own, mmm?

Bernard Yes. Yes, right.

Nanny Ogg What a good boy.

Bernard drags off the body during the following

Mr Bucket and Mr Salzella enter from a different direction, followed by Agnes Nitt, who is supporting Christine

Salzella Supposing he'd come down in the middle of the act?

Seldom Bucket All right, all right. We'll just have to call in the Watch. But they'll have to be discreet.

Salzella Discreet? Have you ever actually met a Watchman?

Seldom Bucket (*seeing the body being dragged off*) Oh dear. Poor Dr Underschaft. He was always so highly strung.

Salzella Never more so than tonight!

Seldom Bucket That was tasteless!

Salzella Tasteless or not, the curtain goes up in two minutes. I'd better go and round up the orchestra. They'll be in the pub over the road.

Seldom Bucket But — all this upset and distress. Will they be capable of playing?

Salzella They never have been, so I don't see why they should start now. They're musicians, Bucket. The only way a dead body would upset them is if it fell in their beer. And even then they'd play if you offered them dead body money.

Salzella exits

Seldom Bucket (*moving to Agnes Nitt*) How is she?

Agnes Nitt She keeps mumbling a bit ...

Nanny Ogg Cup of tea, anyone? Nothing nicer than a nice cup of tea, well, I tell a lie, but there's no bed handy, just my little joke, no offence meant, anyone for a nice cup of tea?

Agnes Nitt looks round in horror

How about you, miss?
Agnes Nitt Er... no thank you. Er ... do you work here?
Nanny Ogg I'm just helping out Mrs Plinge, who has been taken poorly. I'm Mrs Ogg. Don't mind me.

The entr'acte starts up

Seldom Bucket There's the Overture for Act II. Well, if Christine is still unwell, then ...
Agnes Nitt Yes, Mr Bucket?
Seldom Bucket Perhaps we can find you a white ——
Christine Oh dear, what's happened?
Seldom Bucket Are you all right?
Christine I can't disappoint the dear public.
Seldom Bucket Jolly good. I should hurry then. Perdita will help you. Won't you Perdita?
Agnes Nitt Yes. Of course.
Seldom Bucket And you'll be in the chorus — for the duet? Nearby in the chorus?
Agnes Nitt (*with a sigh*) Yes, I know. Come on, Christine.
Christine Dear Agnes ...

Agnes Nitt and Christine exit

Nanny Ogg Tea?
Seldom Bucket Mmm? Oh, no. Thank you. What a brave girl that Christine is.
Nanny Ogg Oh yes. Miraculous recovery, that. Not.

The music fades. Black-out

SCENE 2
The Shades

A dark and threatening street scene

Granny Weatherwax and Mrs Plinge enter

Granny Weatherwax So. Your boy Walter usually sees you home, does he?
Mrs Plinge He's a good boy, Mrs Weatherwax.
Granny Weatherwax I'm sure you're grateful for a strong lad to lean on.
Mrs Plinge They torment him so. They poke fun at him and hide his broom.

They're not bad boys, but they do torment him.

Granny Weatherwax He brings his broom home, does he?

Mrs Plinge He looks after his things. I'm just in here. Much obliged to you.

Granny Weatherwax How will Walter get home now?

Mrs Plinge Oh, he'll sleep at the Opera House. There's loads of places to sleep there.

Granny Weatherwax I expect your Walter sees most of what goes on in the Opera House. (*She takes Mrs Plinge's wrists*) I wonder what your Walter — saw?

A group of thieves enters

Thief There's only two of you, ladies, and there's six of us. There's no use in screaming. Not in the Shades.

Granny Weatherwax Oh dearie, dearie me. Oh please don't hurt us, kind sirs. We are harmless old ladies. Haven't you got mothers?

Thief I 'ad a mother once. Only I think I must 'ave 'et er.

The thieves laugh. Granny Weatherwax draws two large hatpins out of her hat.

The masked and cloaked figure of the Phantom (Walter) appears

There is a short scuffle, during which the Phantom severely wounds each of the thieves. Then he stops, turns to Granny Weatherwax, and bows low

Phantom Ah. Bella Donna.

The Phantom swirls his cloak and exits

Granny Weatherwax Well, I never! (*She looks at the fallen figures*) Dearie, dearie me! I reckon we're goin' to need some nice hot water and some bits of bandage, and a good sharp needle for stitching, Mrs Plinge. We can't let these poor people bleed to death now, can we, even if they do rob old ladies ...

Mrs Plinge I'll pump up the fire and tear up a sheet. Don't know if I can find a needle ...

Granny Weatherwax Oh, of course. I've got one here. It's a bit rusty and blunt. But we shall do the best we can.

One of the fallen figures whimpers at this

Let's do some good.

Black-out

SCENE 3
The Gods

Nanny Ogg is sitting in the balcony on stage as before, with a jar of pickled walnuts. Only one other chair is now occupied

Nanny Ogg (*to the other audience member*) Pickled walnut?

The other audience member puts a hand to their mouth, and exits. Nanny shrugs and eats one of the nuts

After a moment or two, Granny Weatherwax enters and sits

Oh. Hallo, Esme. How did you get on?
Granny Weatherwax You still had the tickets so I had to talk to a man on the door. He should be all right by the morning. Scared everyone off?
Nanny Ogg Yep.
Granny Weatherwax What's been happening?
Nanny Ogg Well, the Duke's sung a long song to say that he must be going and a dead body fell out of the ceiling.
Granny Weatherwax Ah. If you watch dead bodies long enough in the theatre, you can see them move.
Nanny Ogg Not this one. Strangled. Someone's murderin' opera people. I 'ad a quick word with some of the chorus.
Granny Weatherwax Indeed.
Nanny Ogg It's this Ghost they're all talkin' about.
Granny Weatherwax Hmm. Wears one of them black cloaks and a white mask?
Nanny Ogg How did you know that? I mean, I can't imagine who'd want to murder opera people. Except perhaps other opera people. And some of the audience.
Granny Weatherwax I don't believe in ghosts.
Nanny Ogg Oh Esme! You know I've got a dozen of 'em in my house!
Granny Weatherwax Oh, I believe in ghosts. Sad things hanging around going woogy woogy woogy — but I don't believe they kill people or use swords. (*Pause*) Gytha?
Nanny Ogg Yes, Esme?
Granny Weatherwax What does Bella Donna mean?
Nanny Ogg It's the nobby name for Deadly Nightshade, Esme.
Granny Weatherwax I thought so. Huh! The cheek of it!
Nanny Ogg Only, in opera, it means "beautiful woman".
Granny Weatherwax Really? Oh. (*Pause*) Foolishness! There was a couple of cold potatoes and half a herring for her and Walter's supper, you know. Hardly a stick of furniture.

Nanny Ogg Shame.

Granny Weatherwax Mind you, she's a bit richer now. Especially if she sells all them knives and boots and such.

Nanny Ogg It's a cruel world for old ladies.

Granny Weatherwax Especially one as terrified as Mrs Plinge.

Nanny Ogg Well, I'd be frightened too, if I was old and had young Walter to think about.

Granny Weatherwax No, she's really frightened.

Nanny Ogg Why? Because of the Ghost?

Granny Weatherwax Dunno. But I will find out. We've got to get back in here again. And into Box Eight.

Nanny Ogg Crowbar. A number three claw end should do it.

Granny Weatherwax We're not your Nev. Anyway, we've got to have a right to be here.

Nanny Ogg Cleaners. We could be cleaners ...

Granny Weatherwax No, that wouldn't be right. Not with all our — your money. Of course — we could always buy Box Eight.

Nanny Ogg Wouldn't work. They're scared of sellin' it.

Granny Weatherwax Why not? There's people dying and the show still goes on. That lot would sell their own granny for enough money.

Nanny Ogg It's cost a fortune, anyway ... Oh, no, Esme! I was goin' to save that money for me old age! Anyway, we don't look right!

Granny Weatherwax I asked Mrs Plinge. There's an elegant dress emporium just the other side of the river. We'll go there tomorrow.

Nanny Ogg (*with a sigh*) Yes, Esme.

Pause

I'm being punished, ain't I, Esme?

Granny Weatherwax Can't imagine what you're talking about, Gytha.

Nanny Ogg Just 'cos I had my little moment.

Granny Weatherwax I really don't follow you. Anyway, you said you were at your wits' end with thinking what you'd do with the money.

Nanny Ogg Yes, but I'd have quite liked to have been at my wits' end on a comfy chase longyou somewhere with lots of big strong men buyin' me chocolates and pressin' their favours on me.

Granny Weatherwax Money don't buy happiness, Gytha.

Nanny Ogg I only wanted to rent it for a few weeks.

Granny Weatherwax What is it you know, Walter Plinge? What is it you've seen?

Black-out

Christine's Room

Agnes Nitt sits on the bed, holding a mug of warm milk. Christine sweeps back and forth, carrying a bouquet of flowers

Christine Wasn't it amazing?

Agnes Nitt Yes indeed.

Christine Five curtain calls! Mr Bucket says that's more than anyone's had since Dame Gigli!! I'm sure I won't be able to sleep for the excitement!

Agnes Nitt Look, you just have this nice milk drink I've made for you. It took me ages to carry it up from the kitchen. (*She stands and hands it to Christine*)

Christine Yes. Ooh, it tastes ... funny! Have you seen that Walter Plinge?! Isn't he strange?! Have you seen the way he stares at me?! (*She sits on the bed*) Do you think you could find some water for these, Agnes?!

Agnes Nitt Certainly, Christine. It's only seven flights of stairs.

Christine Agnes? Are there spices in this drink? (*And she is asleep*)

A knock at the door

Agnes Nitt Come in, Walter.

Walter Plinge enters, carrying Greebo and some more flowers. He stumbles, and drops the flowers

Walter Plinge Sorry, mu-miss. Oh, what's happened to Miss Christine?

Agnes Nitt I gave her a Lancre herbal drink. She needed a good night's sleep. She's had an exciting day, hasn't she?

Walter Plinge Yes, miss.

Agnes Nitt What else have you got there, Walter?

Walter Plinge It's a kitten. Look!

Agnes Nitt That's Greebo, isn't it?

Walter Plinge He's a happy cat! He's full of milk! Um, well, good-night, miss!

Walter Plinge exits

Agnes Nitt takes the mug off Christine and puts it on the floor. She arranges Christine on the bed

The Phantom's voice (Walter's voice, disguised) comes from off stage

Phantom (*off*) Madam?
Agnes Nitt (*speaking like Christine*) Sir?!
Phantom (*off*) Attend. Tomorrow you must sing the part of Laura in "Il
   Truccatore". We have much to do. One night is barely enough. The aria in
   Act One will occupy much of our time. Your performance tonight was —
   good. But there are areas we must build upon. So: Laura in "Il Truccatore
   (The Master of Disguise)", also sometimes more vulgarly known as "The
   Man of a Thousand Faces"...

Music. Black-out

SCENE 5
Backstage At The Opera

*A few people mill around. André, carrying theatre programmes, talks to one
of the crew*

Seldom Bucket enters and crosses the stage

Walter Plinge enters with some post

Walter Plinge Mr Bouquet! Mr Bouquet!
Seldom Bucket Bucket, Walter, Bucket! Who's dead?
Walter Plinge No-one, Mr Bou ... Mr Bucket! I've got your letters!
Seldom Bucket Oh, thank you Walter.

   Walter Plinge exits

*Seldom Bucket sifts through the post. He spots a particular letter and opens
it*

   Mr Salzella!

The letter appears on the screen:
   "My dear Bucket,
   *I should be most grateful if Christine sings the role of Laura tonight. I
   assure you she is more than capable. The second violin is a little slow, I feel,
   and the second act last night was frankly extremely wooden. May I extend
   my own welcome to Señor Basilica. I congratulate you on his arrival.
   Wishing you the very best,*
   The Opera Ghost."

Salzella enters. He looks at the note

Salzella You don't intend to give in to this?

Seldom Bucket She does sing superbly, Salzella.

Salzella You mean the Nitt girl.

Seldom Bucket Well — yes. But this is blackmail!

Salzella I've been to see Commander Vimes of the City Watch. His men have been here questioning the artistes and staff. He said he'll have some of his best men here tonight. We've got to do this properly. Did you know Dr Underschaft was strangled before he was hung?

Seldom Bucket Hanged. Men are hanged. It's dead meat that's hung.

Salzella Really? I appreciate the information. Well poor Dr Underschaft was strangled apparently. And then he was hung.

Agnes Nitt enters

Seldom Bucket Really, Salzella, you do have a misplaced sense of ...

Salzella I'm afraid it's working here. You have to find some way of dealing with it. Hallo, Perdita.

Agnes Nitt Mr Salzella, Mr Bucket. (*She crosses to André; as she does so*) Hallo, André.

The focus of the lights changes, so that Salzella and Seldom Bucket are in less light, though they stay on stage, talking; Agnes Nitt and André are more brightly lit

The "extras" drift off

André Hallo. You look dead tired. You've missed all the excitement. The Watch have been down here asking lots of questions.

Agnes Nitt What sort of questions?

André Well, knowing the Watch, probably: "Was it you what did it?" They're rather slow thinkers.

Agnes Nitt Oh dear. Does that mean tonight's performance is cancelled?

André (*laughing*) Oh, I don't think Mr Bucket could possibly cancel it. People have been queuing for tickets!

Agnes Nitt Why? Because of Dr Underschaft, you mean? That's disgusting!

André Human nature, I'm afraid. Of course some will be coming to see Señor Basilica. And, of course, Christine is popular too ... oh, sorry.

Agnes Nitt I don't mind, honestly. Um ... how long have you worked here, André?

André Er ... only a few months. I — used to teach music to the Seriph's children in Klatch.

Agnes Nitt And what do you think about the Ghost? Do you know if he sings?

André I heard he sends little critiques to the manager. Some of the girls say they've heard singing in the night. But they're always saying silly things. I mean, they say there are secret passages. They're always saying they've seen the Ghost — sometimes in two places at once! (*He produces some old theatre programmes*) Look, I've got you some old programmes; you might find the notes useful, as you're new to opera. We've got to put all this past us — the show must go on, you know.

Agnes Nitt (*browsing through the programmes*) The show must go on. Everyone says that. The building's on fire – the show must go on. Scenery collapsed? The show must go on. Leading tenor died? Then ask if anyone in the audience knows the part and then they get their big chance while their predecessor's body cools gently in the wings. Why? It's only a performance, for heaven's sake! (*She sees a name in the programme*) Hold on — Walter Plinge? Walter? But ... he doesn't sing, does he?

André What? Oh no! Good heavens. It's a kind of convenient name. Sometimes someone has to sing a minor role — a role they'd rather not be remembered in. Well, here they just go down as Walter Plinge. I suppose it started as a joke.

Agnes Nitt What does Walter think about it?

André I don't think he minds. It's hard to tell, though, isn't it?

There is a crash off stage

Mrs Clamp (*off*) Walter Plinge!

Walter Plinge (*off*) Sorry Mrs Clamp!

Mrs Clamp (*off*) And what's that cat doing in my kitchens?

André It is a little cruel, I suppose. The poor chap is a bit daft.

Agnes Nitt I'm not at all sure that I've met anyone here who isn't. Everyone acts as though it's only the music that matters! The plots don't make sense! Large ladies play the part of consumptive girls! No-one can act! There should be a sign on the door that says "Leave your common sense here". Of course, that's it, isn't it? It's the show that matters, isn't it? It's all show. I — er — I'd better go and practice. (*She heads for the exit*)

André You've really picked up the part of Iodine well.

Agnes Nitt I — er — have a private tutor.

André Then he's really studied opera, that's all I can say.

Agnes Nitt Er ... yes.

Agnes exits

André heads in the opposite direction to Agnes. As he passes Salzella and Seldom Bucket, the Lights brighten on them and we join their conversation

André exits

Salzella It's disgusting. It's pandering to the most depraved taste.

Seldom Bucket I don't like it any more than you do, but it's gone too far. We're completely sold out. The show must go on.

Salzella Oh yes. Would you like me to slit a few throats in the second half? So no-one feels disappointed?

Seldom Bucket Of course not. We don't want any deaths. But ... Anyway, I believe we're past the worst. Where's Señor Basilica?

Salzella Mrs Plinge is showing him to his dressing-room.

Seldom Bucket Mrs Plinge hasn't been murdered?

Salzella No. No-one has today. And it must be, oh, at least ten past twelve. I will go and fetch him, shall I? So that we can have lunch.

Salzella exits

Nanny Ogg pops her head round the door

Nanny Ogg Coo-ee! It's only me!

Seldom Bucket It's — Mrs Ogg, isn't it?

Nanny Ogg I thought I'd better nip round here and warn you.

Seldom Bucket Warn me? What about?

Nanny Ogg Have you ever heard of Lady Esmerelda Weatherwax?

Seldom Bucket No. Should I?

Nanny Ogg Famous patron of the opera. Conservatories all over the place. Pots of money, too.

Seldom Bucket Well, I ——

Nanny Ogg She ain't the sort who likes to be kept waiting. They say she was a famous courtesan in her younger days. Retired now, so they say.

Seldom Bucket You'd better show her up to my office; perhaps I could give her a few minutes.

Nanny Ogg No-one ever gave Lady Esmerelda less than half an hour. (*She winks*) I'll go and fetch her, shall I?

Nanny Ogg exits. Bucket sighs and exits in a different direction. A short pause

Nanny and Granny enter. Granny wears a very smart black evening dress, with jet embroidery

   Esme?

Granny Weatherwax Yes, Gytha?

Nanny Ogg I mean, I'm not complaining or anything — but why isn't it me who's being the posh opera patronizer?

Granny Weatherwax Because you're common as muck, Gytha.

Nanny Ogg Oh. Right. Fair enough.

Granny Weatherwax It's not as though I like this.

Nanny Ogg Um, Esme. I reckon we've spent — prob'ly more than a thousand dollars so far, what with the dress, the manicure and stuff, and that's not including the coach and horses or the rent for the rooms.

Granny Weatherwax You said nothing was too much trouble to help a Lancre girl. Now then, Gytha Ogg, you wouldn't be a witch if you didn't jump to conclusions, so I've no doubt at all that there's some kind if idea floating around in your mind about this Ghost ...

Nanny Ogg Well, sort of an idea, yes.

Granny Weatherwax A name, perhaps?

Nanny Ogg Well — something crossed my mind. A kind of — feeling. I mean, you never can tell.

Granny Weatherwax Yes. It's all neat, isn't it? It's a lie. Like the lie about masks.

Nanny Ogg What lie about masks?

Granny Weatherwax The way people say they hide faces.

Nanny Ogg They do hide faces.

Granny Weatherwax Only the one on the outside.

Black-out

Scene 6
Mr Bucket's Office

Salzella, Enrico Basilica and his Manager are on stage

Seldom Bucket enters

Seldom Bucket Señor Basilica. I trust the dressing rooms are to your satisfaction?

The Manager says something (in "Italian") to Basilica, who replies, also in "Italian"

Manager Señor Basilica says they are fine, but the larder isn't big enough.

Seldom Bucket laughs, a little embarressed

Seldom Bucket Ah, well, I'm sure that Señor Basilica will be very happy to hear that our kitchens have made a special effort ... (*He claps his hands*)

Two stagehands enter and set up a table and chairs

There is a peremptory knock at the door, and Granny Weatherwax enters

Granny Weatherwax Which one of you is Bucket? Ai am Esmerelda Weatherwax.
Seldom Bucket But of course. I am Bucket. No doubt you know Señor Basilica?
Granny Weatherwax Of course. Ai'm sure Señor Basilica recalls the many happy times we've had in other opera houses whose names I can't quite remember for the moment.

Basilica mumbles something to his Manager

Manager Er, Señor Basilica has just said how fondly he recalls meeting you many times before at opera houses that have just slipped his mind at present.
Seldom Bucket Oh, uh, and this is Mr Salzella, our director of music.
Salzella Honoured.
Granny Weatherwax And what's the first thing you'd take out of a burning house, Mr Salzella?
Salzella What would you like me to take, madam?
Granny Weatherwax (*pensively, to herself*) Ah-ha. (*She turns and speaks to Basilica and his Manager*)

Salzella pulls Seldom Bucket to him

Who the hell is she?
Seldom Bucket Apparently she's rolling in money. And very keen on opera.
Salzella Never heard of her.
Seldom Bucket Well Señor Basilica has, and that's good enough for me. Make yourself pleasant to her while I sort out lunch. (*He crosses to the door*)

Seldom Bucket opens the door and Nanny Ogg falls in

Nanny Ogg Sorry! These doorknobs are a bugger to polish, aren't they?
Seldom Bucket Er, Mrs ——
Nanny Ogg Ogg.
Seldom Bucket Ogg, could you please run along to the kitchens and tell Mrs Clamp there will be another one for lunch.
Nanny Ogg Er, that's what I came up to tell you, Mr Bouquet.
Seldom Bucket Bucket.
Nanny Ogg Bucket. There's been a bit of a problem.
Seldom Bucket Who's dead?

Nanny Ogg Oh, no-one's dead. The pasta's gone all black, and they can't get the squid to come down off the ceiling.

Seldom Bucket This is terrible! Please assure Señor Basilica that we will send out for fresh pasta straight away. Um, what were we having, Mrs Ogg?

Nanny Ogg Roast mutton with clootie dumplings. And there's some nice slumpie with butter on it.

Enrico Basilica whimpers and whispers frantically to his Manager

Granny Weatherwax Well, I for one don't believe in pandering to singers. Fancy food indeed! I never heard the like! Why not give him mutton with the rest of us?

Seldom Bucket Oh, Lady Esmerelda, that's no way to ...

Manager Señor Basilica says he would be more than happy to taste the indigenous food of Ankh-Morpork.

Seldom Bucket No, we really can't ...

Manager In fact Señor Basilica insists that he tries the indigenous food of Ankh-Morpork.

Enrico Basilica S'right. Si.

Granny Weatherwax Good. And give him some beer while you're about it.

Enrico Basilica, Nanny Ogg and Granny Weatherwax exchange winks, unseen by the others

Black-out

Scene 7
The Cellars Under The Opera

Water effect. Dripping sounds. Gloomy

Agnes Nitt enters, carrying a candle. We hear her thoughts as Perdita over the speakers

Agnes Nitt What am I doing down here? All right, so there's a secret passage with an entrance between Christine's room and mine. So what?

Perdita (*voice-over*) So what? It's romantic, that's what. It's...thrilling. Be Perdita — forget Agnes. Perdita gets things done.

Agnes Nitt Look, whatever's down there is probably best left where it is.

Perdita (*voice-over*) Say it. You mean the Ghost. He'll have a vast cave somewhere under the Opera House. There'll be hundreds of candles, a dinner table shining with crystal glass and silverware. And of course he'll have a huge organ ——

Agnes Nitt reacts

> — on which, that is to say, he will play in a virtuoso style many opera classics!

Agnes Nitt It'll be damp. There'll be rats.

There is a noise, off

> Er, hallo ...? Um, anyone ...?

Walter Plinge enters, carrying a sack and a lantern. Greebo, in cat form, is supposedly with him, but the audience does not see him

Walter Plinge Hallo, Miss Nitt. What are you doing down here with all the rats, miss?

Agnes Nitt Walter! (*She looks off*) Is that Greebo with you?

Walter Plinge Yes. I got to do poor Mr Pounder's job now he's passed away. No peace for the wicked. Lucky Greebo's bin helping me, haven't you? Come for an explore, have you? These ole tunnels go all the way down to the river.

Agnes Nitt Er, yes. I got lost. Sorry. You have to catch rats as well?

Walter Plinge I am a person of all jobs!

Agnes Nitt Have you ever seen the Ghost, Walter?

Walter Plinge I — er — I saw him in the big room in the ballet school.

Agnes Nitt Really? That's that room with the mirror walls, isn't it. What did he do?

Walter Plinge He ran off! Look, you can't stay here on your own. I'll see you back to your room, OK?

Agnes Nitt Yes. Thank you, Walter. Come on, Greebo.

They exit

Black-out

Scene 8
Mr Bucket's Office

This is set as the end of Scene 6, but with the remains of the main course on the plates. Nanny Ogg, Granny Weatherwax, Seldom Bucket, Enrico Basilica and his Manager are positioned round the table as before. Nanny is clearing the plates

Granny Weatherwax Well, I must say, Señor, I've seen some people pack food away, but you really beat the lot.

Seldom Bucket You were saying that you might be inclined to patronize our opera house.

Granny Weatherwax Oh yes. Is Señor Basilica going to sing tonight?

Salzella I hope so. That or explode.

Granny Weatherwax Then I shall definitely want to be there.

Seldom Bucket Er, seats for tonight are in fact, um ...

Granny Weatherwax A box would do me. I'm not fussy. How about Box Eight? I've heard that Box Eight's always empty.

Seldom Bucket Er, Box Eight, um, er, Box Eight ... er, you see, we don't ——

Granny Weatherwax I was thinking of donating a little something. Two thousand dollars was what I had in mind.

Nanny Ogg crashes the plates

Oh dear.

Seldom Bucket Would you excuse us, please?

Seldom Bucket and Salzella move away. Basilica talks to his Manager

Nanny Ogg Two thousand dollars!

Granny Weatherwax It's only money.

Nanny Ogg It's only money? It's only my money, not only your money!

Granny Weatherwax But, Gytha, I thought you despised riches!

Nanny Ogg Right, so I'd like to get the chance to despise them up close.

Granny Weatherwax I knows you, Gytha Ogg. Money'd spoil you.

Nanny Ogg I'd just like to have the chance to prove that it wouldn't, that's all.

Nanny Ogg stamps off

Salzella and Bucket return to the table

Seldom Bucket Ha, ha. It's laughable, I know, but there are some old theatrical traditions associated with Box Eight, all nonsense, of course — it's haunted, you see ...

Granny Weatherwax just stares at him

Um, well, because of the danger, er, which of course doesn't exist, haha, we — that is the management — feel we should insist, um, that is, politely request, that if you do enter Box Eight you do so in company with a — man.

Granny Weatherwax A man?

Nanny Ogg enters with the chocolate pudding

Seldom Bucket For protection. Um.
Salzella (*to himself*) Although who'd protect him we couldn't say.
Seldom Bucket We thought perhaps one of the staff ...
Granny Weatherwax Ai am quate capable of finding my own man should the need arise.
Nanny Ogg Anyone for pudding? (*She serves it all up*)
Seldom Bucket My word. That looks delicious!
Nanny Ogg It's my own recipe.
Enrico Basilica Mmmm!
Nanny Ogg Lady Weatherwax?
Granny Weatherwax I don't mind if I do.

They eat. The pudding starts to take almost instant "groinal" effect on all, except Enrico and Granny Weatherwax. Nanny Ogg watches with amusement

Manager I'm sure I detect a trace of cinnamon.
Seldom Bucket Indeed, and just a hint of nutmeg.
Salzella I thought — cardamom?
Seldom Bucket Creamy yet spicy. And (*he looks ever-so-slightly uncomfortable*) curiously — warming.

Granny Weatherwax shoots Nanny Ogg a suspicious glance. She is all innocence!

Er, is it me, or is it a trifle warm in here?
Salzella (*gripping his spoon fiercely*) Do you think we could open a window? I feel a little — strange.
Seldom Bucket Yes. By all means.

Salzella starts to rise, then looks embarrassed and sits suddenly

Er — no. I rather believe I'll just sit quietly for a moment.
Manager Oh dear.

Basilica tries to indicate to the Manager that he'd like a bit more of the pudding, but the Manager's thoughts are elsewhere

Oh dear.
Seldom Bucket Er — yes.
Salzella Um, indeed.
Manager Oh dear! Dio Mio! Meus Deus!

Seldom Bucket The weather has been a little — cool of late. Very cold in fact.

Salzella Snow, ice, frost — that sort of thing? Indeed, coldness of all descriptions!

Seldom Bucket Yes, yes!! And at a time like this it is very important to try and remember the names of, say, any number of boring and hopefully chilly things ...

Salzella Wind, glaciers, icicles ——

Seldom Bucket Not icicles! No — no. (*He picks up the water jug, and pours the contents into his lap*) Oh dear! What can I say? I seem to have spilled it all over me. What a butterfingers I am to be sure. Mrs Ogg? Perhaps you could get us another jug.

Manager (*collapsing into his plate*) O-o-oh!

Salzella And quickly please! I, too, am feeling a little accident-prone! In fact, in fact, in fact — I think I shall just — have a brisk ... have a nice cold ... if you would excuse me for a moment.

Salzella leaves hurriedly, in a kind of crouching gait

Seldom Bucket I'll just, I'll just, I'll just — be back quite shortly.

He, too, scurries away

Enrico Basilica stays seated, looking pleased and full. Nanny Ogg crosses to Granny Weatherwax. They start to stack the crockery

Nanny Ogg How much has he had?

Granny Weatherwax Best part of half. But I don't reckon it's taken effect on account of not touching the sides.

Nanny Ogg How about you?

Granny Weatherwax Two helpings.

Nanny Ogg You ain't even sweating! I reckon I'd have to get up real early to put one over on you.

Granny Weatherwax I reckon you should never go to sleep.

Nanny Ogg Sorry, Esme.

Enrico Basilica (*at a loss to follow this conversation*) Absolutely superb. I just loved that pudding, Mrs Ogg. (*He leans back in his chair, puts a hanky over his face, and sleeps*)

Stage hands, including Kevin and Hron, enter and strike the table and chairs during the following

Nanny Ogg He's easy to have around, isn't he? Eat, sleep and sing. You know where you are with him. Esme, how much of my money have we, er, you spent so far?

Granny Weatherwax Don't worry about it, Gytha.

Nanny Ogg If I might say so, Esme, that's very easy for you to say. Oh, I've found Greebo, by the way. He's still following that Walter Plinge around. Say what you like, young Walter's all right with me if Greebo likes him.

Granny Weatherwax Gytha, Greebo would like Norris the Eyeball-Eating Maniac of Quirm if he knew how to put food in a bowl. Now then, about tonight ...

Nanny Ogg I promised Giselle I'd give her a hand with the make-up.

Granny Weatherwax You don't know how to do make-up!

Nanny Ogg I distempered our privvy, didn't I? And I'm helpin' out with the drinks at the swarray. That's a sort of posh party before the opera.

Granny Weatherwax And you haven't done no more special dishes, I trust?

Nanny Ogg Oh no, Esme. Been far too busy for that.

Granny Weatherwax Right. Well, we'd better find Greebo, then. You say he follows Walter about?

Nanny Ogg You sure about this, Esme?

Granny Weatherwax We might have a lot to do tonight. Maybe we could do with an extra pair of hands.

Nanny Ogg Paws.

Granny Weatherwax At the moment, yes.

Black-out

SCENE 9
Backstage At The Opera

Hron and Kevin are crossing the stage with the table from Scene 8. They head for the exit

André enters, carrying some loose sheet music. He passes Kevin and Hron

André Good heavens! Where are you going with that?

Hron Back to the scene dock. Mr Bucket had it in his room for a meal for that new opera singer from Brindisi.

André Señor Basilica, you mean. Oh well, carry on, then.

Hron and Kevin exit with the table

André turns to continue across the stage

Agnes Nitt enters

Agnes Nitt André, André! Can I have a word?

André We've only got a few hours 'til we open, and I'd really ——

Agnes Nitt It's important. I know who the Ghost is.

André pulls Agnes Nitt to one side of the stage

André The Ghost isn't anybody. He's just the Ghost.

Agnes Nitt I mean, he's someone else when he takes off his mask.

André (*sharply*) Who?

Agnes Nitt Walter Plinge. (*Pause*) If you laugh, I'll kick you.

André But Walter isn't even ——

Agnes Nitt I know, but he said he saw the Ghost in the ballet school and there's mirrors all over the walls and he'd be quite tall if he stood up properly — and he roams around in the cellars ...

André Oh, come on ...

Agnes Nitt The other night I heard him singing on the stage when everyone else had gone.

André You saw him?

Agnes Nitt It was dark.

André Oh, well ...

Agnes Nitt But afterwards I'm certain I heard him talking to the cat. Talking normally, I mean. I mean, like a normal person, I mean. And you've got to admit — he is strange. I just thought I'd feel better if I talked to someone about it.

André I wouldn't mention this to anyone else, though. I'll keep an eye on Walter, if you like. But I'd better get on with things.

André exits briskly

Agnes Nitt stands for a moment, lost in thought

Christine enters behind her and taps her on her arm

Agnes Nitt Oh!

Christine It's only me!! What do you think of the dress?!

Agnes Nitt Oh. Yes. very nice.

Christine Well, you don't sound very impressed! Really, Perdita, there's no need to be jealous!!

Agnes Nitt I'm not jealous, I was thinking. I was wondering if Walter Plinge is the Ghost.

Christine But he's a clown!!

Agnes Nitt He walks and talks odd. But if he stood up straight ——

Christine laughs

— and he practically told me he was!

Christine And you believed him, did you?! Really, you girls believe the strangest things!!

Agnes Nitt "You girls"? Good grief! Do you think I'm some sort of impressionable idiot? Think carefully before answering.

Christine Well, of course I don't, but ... I really didn't mean ... look, not Walter — he's just a very odd-job man!

The Phantom (Salzella) enters silently behind them, carrying a silver-topped cane

Agnes Nitt Yes, he does all sorts of jobs! No-one ever knows where he is, they just assume he's ...

Agnes Nitt and Christine turn and see the Phantom. Christine faints — elegantly

It's all right. I know why you're doing it. I really do. You want to be something else and you're stuck with what you are. I know all about that. You're lucky. All you have to do is put on a mask. At least you're the right shape. But why did you have to go and kill people? Why? Mr Pounder can't have done you any harm — unless ... he poked around in odd places, didn't he, and he — found something?

The Phantom nods. He grasps the cane and draws a sword blade out of it

I know who you are! I — I could probably help you! It might not have been your fault! You don't have to be afraid of me!

The Phantom advances on Agnes Nitt

(*Backing off*) I'm your friend, don't you see? Please Walter! Walter!

Walter Plinge (*off*) Miss Nitt? What's the matter? What do you want?

The Phantom hesitates

I'm coming!

The Phantom salutes Agnes Nitt with the sword, sheathes it, bows and exits

Almost immediately, Walter Plinge enters from a nearby entrance with a bucket. He is in evening dress

Agnes Nitt Walter?

Walter Plinge What's the matter with Miss Christine?

Agnes Nitt She — er — she fainted. Probably the — excitement. With the opera. Tonight. Yes, probably. The opera. Um. Excitement, yes.

Walter Plinge Yes. Shall I get the medicine box?

Christine Where am I?

Agnes Nitt You fainted. Why were you nearby, Walter?

Walter Plinge Got to mop out the stagehands' privy, Miss Nitt. Always having trouble with it.

Agnes Nitt But you're in evening dress!

Walter Plinge Yes, then I got to be a waiter afterwards because we're short-handed. Well, I must get on, if you're all right, Miss Christine?

Walter Plinge shuffles off

Agnes Nitt helps Christine up

Agnes Nitt (*to herself*) But he can't have moved that fast. I know the girls say he sometimes seems to be in two places at once, but ... So — the Ghost isn't Walter. And that means — the Ghost must be — someone else. Come on, Christine.

Black-out

Scene 10

The Grand Salon

The stage is busy with extras: audience members, dancers, singers, plus Salzella, Seldom Bucket and Walter Plinge, the last in his waiter's outfit but with beret

Corporal Nobbs (Nobby) and Sergeant Detritus enter and look about them. Nobby is a member of the City Watch; he is shifty, shiftless and looks as though there is more monkey than man in his ancestry. Sergeant Detritus is a troll — a silicaceous life form. Both of them are wearing their Watch uniforms and helmets, with white bow ties and waistcoats and opera cloaks

Sergeant Detritus So. Dis is Opera, eh? Don't forget, Corporal Nobbs, that Commander Vimes said to me, he said: "Sergeant Detritus", he said, "you is to mingle unob-trusiv-lee wiv de flash Opera goers."

Corporal Nobbs Count de Nobbs.

Sergeant Detritus What?

Corporal Nobbs I'm not Corporal Nobbs, I'm the Count de Nobbs. It's my

disguise. And you're the Count de Tritus.
Sergeant Detritus Oh. Yeah.

Nanny Ogg enters with a tray of drinks and crosses to Detritus and Nobbs

Nanny Ogg What can I get you, officers?

During the following dialogue, Corporal Nobbs takes and drinks three sherries off the tray

Sergeant Detritus Officers? Us? What makes you think we're Watchmen?
Nanny Ogg Well, for one thing, he's left his helmet on.
Sergeant Detritus Nah. We're gentlemen of means. Oo'va nuffin whatever to do with the City Watch.
Nanny Ogg Right. Can I get you a drink, then?
Sergeant Detritus No fanks. Not while I'm on duty.

Nanny Ogg moves away

Corporal Nobbs Oh, brilliant. Very undercover that was. "Not while I'm on duty!" Why don't you just wave your truncheon around while you're at it?
Sergeant Detritus Well, if you think it'd help ... Oh, I get it, that was irony, wasn't it. To a superior officer.
Corporal Nobbs Can't be a superior officer, can you — 'cos we ain't Watchmen! Look, let me explain it again ...

Corporal Nobbs and Sergeant Detritus drift off into the crowd

Walter Plinge Want a drink Mr Salzella? There's lots.
Salzella Plinge, you just say, "Drink, sir?". And take off that ridiculous beret!
Walter Plinge My mum made it for me!

Bucket crosses to Salzella, who waves Walter Plinge away

Seldom Bucket Ah, going well, isn't it?
Salzella I suppose so.
Seldom Bucket The Watch are here, you know. In secret. They're mingling.
Salzella Let me guess — you mean that little man with the words "Watchman in Disguise" flashing on and off just above his head?
Seldom Bucket Where? I didn't see that!
Salzella It's Corporal Nobby Nobbs. The only known person to require an identity card to prove his species. I've watched him mingle with three large

sherries. Oh yes, and accompanying him is Sergeant Detritus. These, you understand, are people Commander Vimes selected for their ability to blend in.

Seldom Bucket They'll be very useful if the Gho — oh my gods, what has she found?

Granny Weatherwax enters, with Greebo — in his human, "New Romantic", style

He certainly doesn't look like a gentleman. Lady Esmerelda! How pleasant to see you again! Won't you introduce us to your — guest?

Granny Weatherwax This — is Lord Gribeau. Mr Bucket, the owner, and Mr Salzella, who seems to run the place.

Salzella Hahaha.

Greebo snarls

Haha. Erm, may I order you something?

Granny Weatherwax He'll have milk.

Salzella I expect he has to keep up his strength.

Granny Weatherwax What!

Salzella Nothing.

Nanny crosses to them with a tray of drinks, including a milk

Seldom Bucket Milk? How very foresighted of you.

Nanny Ogg Well, you never know.

Greebo takes the milk and starts to lap at it. Salzella and Bucket stare

Greebo What yourrr lookin' at? Neverrr seein mil-uk drun beforr?

The performance bell sounds

Salzella Never quite like ... well, if you'll excuse us? That was the performance bell. Things to do and so on.

Salzella and Seldom Bucket move off. The rest of the crowd also move off, except Walter Plinge; Nanny Ogg, Granny Weatherwax and Greebo are left behind too

Nanny Ogg What do you think?

Granny Weatherwax He looks like an assassin, but he'll do.

Nanny Ogg Now, you just stay with Granny and do everything she tells you like a good boy.
Greebo Yess, Nan-ny.
Nanny Ogg And no fighting.
Greebo No, Nan-ny.
Nanny Ogg And no leavin' bits of people on the doormat.
Greebo No, Nan-ny.
Nanny Ogg And no turning back into a cat until we say.
Greebo No, Nan-ny.
Granny Weatherwax You behave yourself.
Greebo Yess, Gran-ny.
Granny Weatherwax No going to the lavatory in the corners.

Granny Weatherwax, Nanny Ogg and Greebo drift towards the exit

Greebo (*as they go*) No, Gran-ny.

They exit

Salzella enters and crosses to Walter Plinge

Salzella Walter, come on, the opera is about to start. And don't forget, if you see anything, anything at all, you are to let me know at once.
Walter Plinge We musn't interrupt the opera, Mr Salzella!
Salzella People would understand, I'm sure ...
Walter Plinge The show must go on, Mr Salzella!
Salzella Walter, I ... Look, let's just catch the Ghost. Of course I don't want to stop the show. Now come on.

Black-out

SCENE 11
The Corridor Behind The Boxes

A champagne bottle is to hand

Mrs Plinge is on stage, just coming out of Box Eight, with a dustpan and brush

Nanny Ogg enters

Nanny Ogg Evenin', Mrs Plinge!
Mrs Plinge Oh, hallo, Mrs Ogg.
Nanny Ogg Certainly very packed tonight. (*Pointedly*) Every seat sold, I hear.

This does not get the required reaction

Shall I give you a hand cleaning out Box Eight?

Mrs Plinge I just done it, Mrs Ogg.

Nanny Ogg Yes, but I heard that her ladyship is very particular. Very picky about things.

Mrs Plinge What ladyship?

Nanny Ogg Mr Bucket has sold Box Eight, you see.

Mrs Plinge Aah! But he can't do that!!

Nanny Ogg It's his Opera House. I s'pose he thinks he can.

Mrs Plinge It's the Ghost's box!

Nanny Ogg I shouldn't think he'll mind for just one night. The show must go on, eh? You all right, Mrs Plinge?

Mrs Plinge I think I should just go and ... (*She moves to exit*)

Nanny Ogg stops Mrs Plinge

Nanny Ogg (*suddenly forceful*) No, you have a good sit down and a rest.

Mrs Plinge But I should go and ——

Nanny Ogg And what, Mrs Plinge? I expect you wanted to go and have a word with somebody, did you Mrs Plinge? Someone who might be a little shocked to find his box full, perhaps? I reckon I could put a name to that someone, Mrs Plinge. Now if ——

Mrs Plinge grabs the champagne bottle and moves to strike Nanny Ogg with it, but Nanny is too quick and grabs her arm, putting her other hand over Mrs Plinge's mouth

Year of the Insulted Goat's a good year. You don't want to try and outsmart me, Mrs Plinge. You just wait here quietly with me. And don't go thinking I'm nice. I'm only nice compared with Esme, but so's ev'ryone.

Mrs Plinge Mmmf!

Nanny Ogg Y'see, the thing about Esme is she's stupid ——

Mrs Plinge Mmf?

Nanny Ogg — so she thinks that the most obvious way for the Ghost to get in and out of the box is through the door. If you can't find a secret panel, she says, it's because there ain't one. And a secret panel that ain't there is the best sort, the reason being, no bugger can find it. That's where you people think all operatic, see? You can't see a trapdoor so you say "What a hidden trapdoor it must be". The best way for a Ghost to get around the place without being seen is for him to be seen but not noticed. Especially if he's got keys. People don't notice Walter.

Nanny Ogg takes her hand from Mrs Plinge's mouth

Don't worry. Esme'll help you if she can.

Mrs Plinge What if she can't?

Nanny Ogg Do you think Walter did those murders?

Mrs Plinge No! He's a good boy! They'll put him in prison.

Nanny Ogg If he done them murders, Esme won't let that happen.

Mrs Plinge Well that's very ... What do you mean, she won't let it happen?

Nanny Ogg I mean, that if you throw yourself on Esme's mercy, you'd better be damn sure you deserve to bounce.

Black-out

SCENE 12
Box Eight

Greebo sits in the balcony, illuminated by the glow from the stage

Walter Plinge enters into a follow spot outside the balcony. He removes his beret and pockets it. He puts on the Ghost's mask and straightens, becoming perceptibly taller and more noble. He puts on the hat and cloak and exits

Moments later he enters the box and sits in the third seat

Greebo You carrrn't have my fissh eggs!

Walter Plinge leaps to his feet and turns to leave

   Granny Weatherwax enters the box and blocks Walter Plinge's way

Granny Weatherwax Well, well, we meet again.

Walter Plinge backs to the edge of the box rail and looks down

   I shouldn't think you can jump, it's a long way down. Now, Mr Ghost ...

Walter Plinge clambers on to the rail, climbs over the edge and jumps down out of view

   Greebo!

Greebo Yess, Granny!

Granny Weatherwax Catch him! And there could be a kipper in it for you!

Greebo Thiss is more like it! Opera is borrring! Chasing things – that's what cats do best!

Greebo follows Walter Plinge over the rail

The Lights cross-fade to the theatre

Walter Plinge, pursued by Greebo, exits through the auditorium

Nanny Ogg enters into a different part of the theatre

Nanny Ogg Stay there, Mrs Plinge! What's happening? Oh, I get it —
something's gone wrong. I bet Esme's tried her famous stare and it hasn't
worked, what with it being so gloomy and him in his mask.

*Salzella enters, brandishing a mask. More people enter; Agnes Nitt and
Colette are with them*

Salzella It was Plinge! Quick! get after him!
Colette Walter?
Salzella Yes, Colette, Walter!

Kevin and Hron enter from the auditorium

Kevin I saw the Ghost heading up to the roof! And there was some big one-
eyed bastard going after him like a scalded cat!
Nanny Ogg Eh? You what?
Salzella To the roof!
Hron Hadn't we better get flaming torches first?
Kevin Yeah, and pitchforks and scythes.
Salzella That's just for vampires. Get on with it!

A small group rushes off into the auditorium

Colette, Agnes and Salzella remain

Giselle and Solange enter

Giselle What's happening?
Salzella They've got the Ghost! He's heading for the roof! It's Walter
Plinge!
Solange What, Walter? Our Walter Plinge?
Salzella Yes!

Salzella rushes off

Giselle Walter? Surely not!
Solange We-ell: he's a bit odd, isn't he?
Colette And he's always around the place!

Agnes Nitt It's not Walter.
Colette But that's who he said they were chasing!
Agnes Nitt I don't know who they're chasing, Colette, but Walter's not the Ghost! He wouldn't hurt a fly! How could you think otherwise?
Colette Come on, or we'll miss everything!
Agnes Nitt No, wait! You mustn't! It isn't Walter! (*ad lib*)

Salzella, Giselle, Solange, Colette et al exit through the auditorium

Agnes Nitt remains on stage, protesting. The Lights cross-fade to the roof of the Opera House. Star gobo on sky. Wind noise

Walter Plinge, as the Phantom, clambers into view. Suddenly, Granny Weatherwax appears and whips the mask from Walter Plinge's face. Instantly, he dwindles down into Walter Plinge again

Greebo enters

Granny Weatherwax Good-evening, Walter.
Walter Plinge Hallo, Missus Weatherwax!
Granny Weatherwax Mistress. Now stand up properly.

Walter Plinge makes an effort to stand up straight

Nice up here on the opera roof, ain't it? There's fresh air and stars. I thought: he'll go up or down, but there's only rats down.

Granny Weatherwax grabs Walter Plinge by the chin and stares into his eyes

How does your mind work, Walter Plinge? If your house was on fire, what's the first thing you'd try to take out?
Walter Plinge The fire!
Granny Weatherwax You're daft, Walter Plinge.
Walter Plinge Daft as a broom, Mistress Weatherwax!
Granny Weatherwax But you ain't insane. You're daft but you're sane. There's worse things than that. Well done, Walter. A good answer. Greebo!

Greebo nudges Walter Plinge heavily in the back

Greebo Want milluk right noaow! Purrrrr!

Granny Weatherwax thrusts the mask at Greebo

Granny Weatherwax You put this on! And you stay down real low, Walter
Plinge. One man in a mask is pretty much like another, after all.

Walter moves out of sight behind the small curtains, huddling on the floor

And when they chase you, Greebo — give them a run for their money. Do
it right and there could be a —
Greebo Yurrr, I knoaow. Lot of work for one kipper.
Granny Weatherwax And Greebo, if you're cornered and have to turn back
into a cat, make sure you leave them the mask. Understand?
Greebo Yessss, Grannnn-y.

*A small crowd enters at "ground level"; Kevin, Hron, Corporal Nobbs,
Sergeant Detritus and Nanny Ogg are among them. Granny Weatherwax
moves out of sight*

Kevin Look! There he is! Up there, near the dome!
Greebo (*adopting a threatening posture*) Woowrrr!

Greebo disappears from view

Hron We'd, er, better get after him, then.
Kevin We'd better get after him by carefully going down the back stairs, you
mean?
Hron There's only one of him, and there's lots of us, right? Look, at worst
he'd only be able to get one or two of us...
Kevin Oh. That's good, is it?
Hron No, come on, let's get him! Come on!

The crowd, muttering to themselves, move off

*Nanny is left, looking the opposite way, and Walter Plinge is still behind the
small curtains*

Nanny (*muttering*) Rhubarb, rhubarb ...

Granny enters, goes up to Nanny and taps her on her shoulder

Granny Weatherwax They've gone, Gytha.
Nanny Ogg Rhuba... oh, hallo, Esme. I was just tagging along to see it didn't
get out of hand. Was that Greebo I saw?
Granny Weatherwax Yes.
Nanny Ogg Aww, bless 'im. He looked a bit bothered, though. I hope he
doesn't "happen" to anyone.

Granny Weatherwax Now, look here, Gytha. (*She goes* US *and pulls aside the curtain*)

Walter Plinge is revealed, huddled on the floor

I'm going to keep an eye on the chase. You'd better look after Walter; you're better at that kind of thing.

Walter Plinge (*mournfully*) Hallo Mrs Ogg!

Nanny Ogg So is he the ... ?

Granny Weatherwax Yes.

Nanny Ogg You mean he really did do the mur —?

Granny Weatherwax What do you think?

Nanny Ogg No.

Granny Weatherwax Right.

Granny Weatherwax follows the crowd off

Nanny Ogg Up you get, Walter. We'd better find somewhere where you can hide out.

Walter Plinge I know a hidden place, Mrs Ogg! (*He crosses to the trapdoor to the cellar and opens it*)

Nanny Ogg That? It doesn't look very hidden to me, Walter.

Walter Plinge It's hidden where everyone can see it, Mrs Ogg!

Nanny Ogg Like you, eh, Walter? This is just an old staircase, is it?

Walter Plinge Yes! It goes all the way down! Except at the bottom it goes all the way up!

Nanny Ogg Anyone else know about it?

Walter Plinge The Ghost, Mrs Ogg!

Nanny Ogg Oh yes. And where's the Ghost now, Walter?

Walter Plinge He ran away!

Nanny Ogg What does the Ghost do here, Walter?

Walter Plinge He watches over the Opera!

Nanny Ogg That's very kind of him, I'm sure. Come on, then.

Walter Plinge You go first, Mrs Ogg. So I will not see your drawers!

Nanny Ogg Er, well, thank you, Walter. (*She starts to enter the trapdoor*)

Black-out

Voices (*off; in the dark*) There he is! This way! Come back, you coward! (*and so on*)

The Lights come up dimly

Greebo enters, looking about him in a hunted manner

Voice (*off; from the wings*) I saw him go through here. Careful!

Greebo moves C

> *A crowd, including Corporal Nobbs and Sergeant Detritus, (and with one crowd member secretly carrying the Greebo cat) enters, sees it is close to Greebo, and backs up to the entrance again*

> *Greebo snarls at the crowd; the crowd roars and charges in at him. There is a mêlée; we can't see what's happening, but in fact the actor sheds his "cat" face and mask and dons a cloak and hat from one of the crowd. The Greebo cat is placed on stage*

Crowd Member He's gone!

The crowd parts and—Greebo the man has "disappeared". The cat whizzes off into the wings

> *The crowd disperses and exits*

Corporal Nobbs and Sergeant Detritus are left on stage

Sergeant Detritus Commander Vimes isn't going to like this. You know he hates it when prisoners disappear.
Corporal Nobbs "The suspect was beaten to death by the crowd and thrown into the Ankh before me and Sergeant Detritus could intervene."
Sergeant Detritus Shouldn't there be some blood? 'Cos if humans is hit hard enough, they leaks all over the place.
Corporal Nobbs No, look, that's just what we'll put in the report. Most important thing now is to get ourselves outside a big drink. Come on.

> *They exit*

> *Agnes Nitt enters in costume and sees Sergeant Detritus and Corporal Nobbs go*

> *Granny Weatherwax enters behind Agnes Nitt*

Agnes Nitt turns to exit but finds her way blocked by Granny Weatherwax

Agnes Nitt Oh. Sorry.
Granny Weatherwax That's all right. It was just my foot. So —how is life in the big city, Agnes Nitt?

Agnes Nitt I'm not Agnes here, actually.

We hear the muffled noise of the overture starting

Look, I've got to go. I'll be needed on stage soon.

Granny Weatherwax It's a good job, is it? Being someone else's voice?

Agnes Nitt I'm doing what I want to. And you can't stop me!

Granny Weatherwax But you ain't part of it, are you? You try, but you always find yourself watchin' other people, eh? Never quite believin' anything.

Agnes Nitt Shut up!

Granny Weatherwax I thought so.

Agnes Nitt I have no intention of becoming a witch, thank you very much!

Granny Weatherwax Now, don't go getting upset just because you know it's going to happen. A witch you're going to be because a witch you are, and if you turn your back on him now then I don't know what's going to happen to Walter Plinge.

Agnes Nitt I knew he was the Ghost. But then I saw he couldn't be.

Granny Weatherwax Ah. Believed the evidence of your own eyes, did you? In a place like this? What do you know?

Agnes Nitt I know he's the Ghost.

Granny Weatherwax Right.

Agnes Nitt And I know he doesn't mean any harm.

Granny Weatherwax Good. Well done. Walter may not know his right from his left but he does know his right from his wrong. So, we know Walter didn't do the murders, so we've just got to find out who did.

Agnes Nitt All right. I'll help if I can. When I'm not on stage, of course. But afterwards — that's it! Afterwards you'll leave me alone. Promise?

Granny Weatherwax Certainly.

Agnes Nitt Well, all right then ... Oh no. That was too easy. I don't trust you.

Granny Weatherwax You don't trust me? It's Nanny Ogg who thinks we ought to have a third witch, not me. I reckon life's difficult enough without some girl cluttering up the place just because she thinks she looks good in a pointy hat.

Agnes Nitt I'm not falling for that one, either. It's where you say I'm too stupid to be a witch and I say, oh no, I'm not, and you end up winning again. I'd rather be someone else's voice than some old witch with no friends and have everyone frightened of me and be nothing more than just a bit cleverer than other people and not do any real magic at all.

Granny Weatherwax Seems to me you're so sharp you might cut yourself. All right. When it's all over, I'll let you go your own way. I won't stop you. Now, nip along to Mr Bucket's office and fetch me his accounts books.

Agnes Nitt But ——

Granny Weatherwax Go on!

Black-out. The music fades

SCENE 13
The Phantom's Lair

*The small curtains open on to Walter Plinge's lair. There is a table with piles
of papers. A small organ or similar with music manuscripts. Lit candles.
Stage props (masks,weapons, shields — whatever)*

Walter Plinge enters with Nanny Ogg

Walter Plinge I found this, Mrs Ogg! It's the Ghost's secret lair!
Nanny Ogg Secret lair, eh? And is the Ghost here, Walter?
Walter Plinge No!
Nanny Ogg Oh my. Oh my, my. It's a harmonium, isn't it? A sort of small
 organ? (*She crosses to it and picks up some of the music manuscripts*)

We hear the overture start in the distance

 An opera about cats? Never heard of an opera about cats. Then again, why
 not? "Guys and Trolls"? "Miserable Les"? Who's he? What are all these,
 Walter?
Walter Plinge (*looking up; with a gasp*) The show's started!

*Nanny Ogg sits at the harmonium and picks up a single sheet of manuscript.
Walter Plinge snatches it from her*

Walter Plinge That one's not finished, Mrs Ogg!
Nanny Ogg Come on, Walter, let me see. I'm sure your mam wouldn't want
 to hear that you'd been a bad boy, would she?

*Walter hands over the sheet. Nanny Ogg looks at it and picks out a few notes
on the "harmonium". (It sounds very like a certain "Phantom" theme)*

 Hey. This is about a smart and debonair Ghost who lives in an opera house.
 I wonder why the Ghost wrote this, eh, Walter?
Walter Plinge There's going to be a lot of trouble, Mrs Ogg.
Nanny Ogg Oh, me and Granny Weatherwax will sort it out.
Walter Plinge It's wrong to tell lies.
Nanny Ogg Prob'ly. Er — what sort of lies would it be wrong to tell, Walter?
Walter Plinge Lies — about things you see. Even if you did see them! He

said our mam would lose her job if I said, Mrs Ogg!

Nanny Ogg Did he? Who?

Walter Plinge The Ghost, Mrs Ogg!

Nanny Ogg Was this the Ghost that wrote all this music, Walter?

Walter Plinge It's wrong to tell lies about the room with sacks in, Mrs Ogg! He said I wasn't to tell anyone!

Nanny Ogg The Ghost? But you're ... Ah, but I ain't anyone. In fact, he prob'ly meant to say "Don't tell anyone except Mrs Ogg", only he forgot. Where are these sacks, Walter?

Walter Plinge indicates an adjoining room. Nanny Ogg exits, and enters with a sack of money

What is this, Walter?

Walter Plinge The Ghost's money!

Nanny Ogg There's a lot of money in there, Walter. I 'spose if I was to ask you, you'd say the Ghost put it there?

Walter Plinge Yes, Mrs Ogg!

Nanny Ogg Walter, you'd better just stay here. I reckon I need to talk to some people. You'll stay here?

Walter Plinge Yes, Mrs Ogg.

Nanny Ogg Good boy.

Nanny Ogg exits

Black-out

A Light comes up in the balcony

The Phantom (Salzella) enters, carrying a gleaming knife. He crosses to a stout rope and shakes it. The chandelier over the audience shudders. The Phantom laughs, and starts to work away at the rope with his knife, with the chandelier shuddering as he does so

Black-out

Scene 14
Back Stage at the Opera

We can hear the sound of the opera in progress

Granny Weatherwax is on stage

Agnes Nitt enters, carrying some ledgers

Agnes Nitt This is all wrong, Granny Weatherwax.

Granny Weatherwax This only looks wrong. You keep a look-out, my girl. (*She riffles through the accounts*)

Agnes Nitt Look, I really ought to go. I'm on stage soon. What're you doing?

Granny Weatherwax Amazin'. Some things entered twice. And I reckon there's a page here where someone's added the month and taken away the time of day.

Agnes Nitt I thought you didn't like books.

Granny Weatherwax I don't. They can look you right in the face and still lie. How many fiddle players in the band?

Agnes Nitt There are nine violinists in the orchestra.

Granny Weatherwax Well, there's a thing. Seems twelve of them are drawing wages, but three of 'em is over the page, so's you mightn't notice. Even Nanny ain't this bad at numbers. To be this bad at numbers you got to be good. No wonder this place never makes any money.

Agnes Nitt There's someone coming!

Granny Weatherwax sinks back into the scenery

André enters

André Agnes! And what the hell are you doing here? You're on stage in five minutes!

Agnes Nitt And what about you? Creeping around! Why aren't you in the orchestra pit?

André Don't meddle in things that don't concern you, girl.

Agnes Nitt Don't speak to me like that! For all I know, you might be the Ghost! We were on important business.

André We?

Granny Weatherwax (*stepping out from her hiding-place*) Yes. We. Now then, young man. I know you ain't the Ghost, so what are you, to be sneaking around in places where you shouldn't be?

André I could ask you the ——

Granny Weatherwax Me? I'm a witch. And I'm pretty good at it.

Agnes Nitt She's from Lancre. Where I come from ...

André Oh? Not the one who wrote that book? I've heard people talking ...

Granny Weatherwax No! I'm much worse than her. Understand?

Agnes Nitt She is.

André I — er — hang around in dark places looking for trouble.

Granny Weatherwax Really? There's a nasty name for people like that.

André Yes. "Policeman".

Granny Weatherwax You don't look like one.

André hands Granny Weatherwax a police badge

Secret policeman?

André There aren't many of us. We've only just started. They needed watchmen who could look for ... hidden crimes.

Granny Weatherwax If your house was on fire, what's the first thing you'd take out of it?

André Who set fire to it?

Granny Weatherwax You're a policeman all right. You come to arrest poor Walter?

André I know he didn't kill Underschaft. I was watching him. He was trying to unblock privies all afternoon. I was almost sure it was Salzella. I'm sure he's stealing money. But the Ghost has been seen when Salzella is perfectly visible, so ...

Granny Weatherwax And how would you recognize this Ghost, Mr Policeman?

André Well, he wears this mask ...

Granny Weatherwax Hang on. Now say it again and think about it. You can recognize him because he's got a mask on? You recognize him because you don't know who he is? Life isn't neat. Whoever said there was only one Ghost?

They exit

The Lights cross-fade to the balcony, where the opera music is louder. The Phantom (Salzella) is still sawing away at the rope

Nanny Ogg enters and holds on to the rope

Nanny Ogg Hallo, Mr Ghost! Keeping busy? Oh, nice view of the opera from up here, ain't there?

The Phantom also holds the rope and holds the knife out towards Nanny. The chandelier rocks, perilously

Millions of people knows I'm up here! You wouldn't hurt a little old lady, would you? Come back to finish it, have you? Make you happy, would it, the whole place burning down?

Seldom Bucket and a couple of stage hands enter at ground level

Seldom Bucket Look! Look! Up there! The Ghost! He's trying to bring down the chandelier! Stop the show! Someone will get hurt. Stop the performance!

The Phantom reacts. He throws the knife at Nanny Ogg and runs off. She follows

Quick! Get out there and stop the show! The rest of you — follow that Ghost!

They all exit

Black-out

SCENE 15
The Phantom's Lair

Walter Plinge sits on stage

We hear the opera performance stop

Walter Plinge reacts violently and leaps to his feet as if scalded

Walter Plinge Nooo!

Granny Weatherwax enters

It's stopped! It's stopped! It's bad luck to stop the show!

Granny Weatherwax Someone better start it again. Mr Salzella is trying to stop the show, isn't he Walter?

Walter Plinge "You haven't seen anything, Walter Plinge! And if you tell lies you will be locked up and I'll see to it that there's big trouble for your mother!"

Granny Weatherwax He found out about the Ghost, didn't he? And he thought: I can use that. But we've got to sort it all out. The trouble is, you see, that if you know right from wrong you can't choose wrong. You just can't do it and live. So ... if I was a bad witch I could make Mr Salzella's muscles turn against his bones and break them where he stood — if I was bad. But I can't do it. That wouldn't be right. (*She pulls out a Phantom mask*) Simple thing, ain't it? Wizard would tell you there's nothing magic about it, and just shows how little they know, eh Walter?

Granny Weatherwax hands the mask to Walter Plinge. He dons it and rises — the Phantom

I don't know what you are when you're behind that mask, but Ghost is just another word for spirit and spirit's just another word for soul. Off you go, Walter Plinge.

He doesn't move

Sorry. Off you go, Ghost. The show must go on. Make sure it does!

Walter Plinge nods and exits

(*Clapping her hands together*) Right! Let's do some good!

Black-out

SCENE 16
On Stage

In the dark we hear part of a tenor aria being sung, then suddenly interrupted. The Lights come up

The cast of the opera are on stage in costume, with Salzella, still wearing his cloak and "Phantom" hat, and Seldom Bucket. Granny Wetherwax is behind the small curtains

Agnes and André burst on

Seldom Bucket I'm sorry, ladies and gentlemen, for this inconvenience ——
André Salzella! You're nicked, me old beauty!

Salzella grabs Agnes Nitt and draws the sword from his sword-stick

Salzella Oh dear oh dear oh dear. How extremely operatic of me. And now, I fear, I shall have to take this girl hostage. Isn't anyone going to say: "You won't get away with this"?
André You won't get away with this.
Salzella You'll have the place surrounded, I have no doubt?
André Yes, we have the place surrounded. I have Corporal Nobbs and Sergeant Detritus out there and when it come to standing in doorways, they're the best.

Christine screams and faints

Salzella Now there's someone operatic! But you see, I am going to get away with it, because I don't think operatically. Myself and this young lady are going down to the cellars where I may possibly leave her unharmed. By now, someone should have said "But why, Salzella?" Honestly, do I have to do everything around here?
Seldom Bucket That's what I was going to say.
Salzella Ah good. Well, in that case, I should say something like: "Because

I wanted to." Because I rather like money, you see. But more than that (*he takes a deep breath*) I really hate opera. I don't want to get needlessly excited about this, but opera, I am afraid, really is dreadful. And I have had enough. So while I have the stage, let me tell you what a wretched, self-adoring, totally unrealistic, worthless art form it is, what a terrible waste of fine music, what a ——

A dramatic chord. The Lights change

Walter enters, as the Phantom. He bows slightly

Salzella thrusts Agnes Nitt away

That is what opera does to a man. It rots the brain, you see, and I doubt whether he had too much of that to begin with. It drives people mad, d'you see. Mad, d'you hear me, mad! Ahahaha!!!!! (*He recovers himself*) Ahem. You don't know what it's been like, being the only sane man in this madhouse! You believe anything! You prefer to believe a Ghost can be in two places at once than that there might simply be two people! Pounder realized. He thought he could blackmail me! Well, of course, I had to kill him for his own good! (*He lashes out with his sword*) And now I'll fight your Ghost. And you'll see that this Ghost of yours doesn't actually know how to fence, because he only knows stage fencing, you see, where the whole point is simply to hit the other fellow's sword with a nice metallic clang — and then to die merely because he's thrust a sword under your armpit! (*Suddenly he reaches forward and pulls off Walter Plinge's mask*) Really, Walter. You are a bad boy!

Walter Plinge Sorry, Mr Salzella!

Salzella Look how everyone's staring!

Walter Plinge Sorry, Mr Salzella!

Salzella See, company? This is your luck! This is your Ghost! Without his mask he's just an idiot who can hardly tie his shoelaces! Ahahaha! Ahem. It's your fault, Walter Plinge...

Walter Plinge Yes, Mr Salzella.

Salzella and Walter are now L *and* R *of the small curtains*

Granny Weatherwax (*off*) No.

The small curtains open to reveal Granny Weatherwax, C, *in witch's hat*

No-one would believe Walter Plinge. Even Walter gets confused about the things he sees.

Salzella Well, well. Lady Esmerelda, eh?

Granny Weatherwax I've stopped bein' a lady, Mr Salzella.

Salzella So now you are a witch instead?

Granny Weatherwax Yes, indeed.

Salzella But this is a sword. Everyone knows you can't magic iron and steel. Get out of the way!! (*He thrusts forward with his sword*)

Granny Weatherwax catches the sword by the blade. Salzella tugs at it, but she holds firm

Granny Weatherwax Tell you what, Mr Salzella — it ought to be Walter Plinge who finishes this, eh? It's him you harmed. Apart from the ones you murdered, of course. You didn't need to do that — but you wore a mask, didn't you? Masks conceal one face, but they reveal another. The one that only comes out in darkness. I bet you could do just what you liked, behind a mask ...?

Salzella tugs again at the sword. Still Granny holds firm. Some of the chorus react to this

Put your mask on, Walter.

Walter Plinge Don't have one any more, Mistress Weatherwax.

Granny Weatherwax Oh, dearie, dearie me. Look at me, Walter. You — trust Perdita, don't you Walter?

Walter Plinge Yes, Mistress Weatherwax.

Granny Weatherwax That's good. Because she's got a new mask for you. A magic one. It's just like your old one, d'you see, only you wear it under your skin and you don't have to take it off and no-one but you will ever know it's there. Got it, Perdita?

Agnes Nitt But I — er, oh, yes. Here it is. In my hand.

Granny Weatherwax You're holding it the wrong way up, my girl.

Agnes Nitt Oh. Sorry.

Granny Weatherwax Now. Take it, Walter.

Walter Plinge takes the invisible mask from Agnes Nitt

Put it on. You do believe there's a mask there, don't you, Walter? Perdita's sensible and she knows an invisible mask when she sees one.

Walter Plinge puts the mask on, and straightens up, smiling faintly

Good. (*To Salzella*) I reckon you two should fight again. But it can't be said I'm unfair. I expect you've got a Ghost mask somewhere? Mrs Ogg saw

you waving it earlier, and she's not as gormless as she looks.
Nanny Ogg Thank you.

Salzella puts on his mask

Granny Weatherwax Right. Now. (*She lets go of the sword*) Now whoever
you are can fight whoever he is.

*Walter Plinge draws a sword from his broom. Salzella and Walter Plinge
fence — but it is a stage fight*

Salzella This isn't fighting! This is ——

*Walter Plinge lunges and catches Salzella under the arm. He staggers
around, drops on one knee, stands again, and staggers to* C .

Whatever happens ... it can't be worse than a season of opera! I don't mind
where I'm going so long as there are no fat men pretending to be thin boys
... Ah — ah — argh! (*He slumps to the floor*)
Agnes Nitt But Walter didn't ——
Nanny Ogg Shut up.
Salzella (*getting up again*) Incidentally, another thing I can't stand about
opera — are the plots. They make no sense! And no-one ever says so! And
the quality of the acting? It's non-existent! Everyone stands around
watching the person who's singing. Ye gods, it's going to be a relief to put
all that behind ... Ah — argh ——(*He slumps to the floor*)
Nanny Ogg Is that it?
Granny Weatherwax Shouldn't think so.
Salzella (*getting up again*) As for the people who attend the opera — I think
it's just possible that I hate them even worse! They're so ignorant! There's
hardly any of them who knows the first thing about music! They come in
here and they leave their intelligence on a nail by the door!
Agnes Nitt Then why don't you just leave? If you've stolen all this money
why didn't you just go away somewhere, if you hate it so much?
Salzella Leave? Leave the opera? ... Argh — argh ——(*He falls to the floor*)
André Is he dead yet?
Agnes Nitt How can he be dead? Good grief, can't anyone see ——
Salzella (*rising again*) You know what really gets me down? It's the way that
in opera everyone takes such a long — time — to — argh! (*He falls again.
For the last time!*)
Nanny Ogg Yep. That's it. Looks like he's gone down for the final curtain
call.
Agnes Nitt But Walter didn't stab him! Why won't anyone listen? Look, the
sword isn't even sticking in him!

Nanny Ogg Yep. Pity no-one told him.

Agnes Nitt But he's dead!

Nanny Ogg Got a bit over-excited, perhaps.

Seldom Bucket He's really dead?

Granny Weatherwax Seems to be. One of the best operatic deaths ever, I should expect.

Seldom Bucket But where's all the money?

Granny Weatherwax In the cellar. Walter'll show you.

Walter Plinge (*now suave and urbane*) I should be delighted.

Granny Weatherwax And since you're going to need a new director of music, you could do worse than young Walter here.

Seldom Bucket Walter?

Granny Weatherwax He knows everything there is to know about opera ...

Nanny Ogg And you should see the music he's written.

Granny Weatherwax Brilliant.

Seldom Bucket Walter?

Granny Weatherwax Walter.

Nanny Ogg Walter.

Seldom Bucket Want to be the director of music, Walter?

Walter Plinge (*now well-spoken*) Thank you, Mr Bucket.

Seldom Bucket Bouquet. Oh.

Walter Plinge Thank you, Mr Bucket. But who'll clean the privies? I won't have to stop doing them, will I? I've just got them working.

Seldom Bucket Oh. Right. Yes. No, of course. You can sing while you do it, if you like. And I won't even cut your pay. I'll — I'll raise it! Six — no, seven shiny dollars!

Walter Plinge Mr Bucket ——

Seldom Bucket Yes, Walter?

Walter Plinge I think — you paid Mr Salzella forty dollars.

Seldom Bucket Is he some kind of monster?

Nanny Ogg Writes brilliant music. Look (*she draws some music out of her clothes; reading*) "Don't cry for me, Scrote". Very sad, that one.

Seldom Bucket Good. Well — good.

André (*looking at the music*) Hey, this is good. Do you know, Mr Bucket, this isn't opera? There's music and — yes, dancing and singing all right, but it's not opera. A long way from opera.

Seldom Bucket How far? You don't mean — you don't mean that it's just possibly that you put music in and you get money out?

André This could very well be the case, Mr Bucket.

Seldom Bucket (*putting one arm round André and one round Walter Plinge*) Good! This calls for a very lar... for a medium-sized drink!

Seldom Bucket, André and Walter exit. The extras start to drift off

Granny Weatherwax, Agnes Nitt and Nanny Ogg stay, and Christine lingers behind

Agnes Nitt Is that it?

Granny Weatherwax Yep.

Agnes Nitt But no-one said thank you, or anything.

Granny Weatherwax Often the case.

Agnes Nitt But what about me?

Nanny Ogg I expect we'd better be getting along, Esme.

Granny Weatherwax The audience haven't gone, you know. They're still sittin' out there ...

Nanny Ogg Can't think why. He told 'em the show was over.

Granny Weatherwax Ah, but it ain't. You see, an opera's not over till ... (*To Agnes*) You feeling a bit peeved?

Agnes Nitt Yes.

Nanny Ogg Feeling a bit forgotten about?

Agnes Nitt Yes.

Granny Weatherwax Best thing is just to give vent to that sort of feeling.

Agnes screams — a long, sustained note

Nanny Ogg Ah. Now the opera's over! Coming with us, Perdita?

Agnes Nitt sighs, shakes her head and runs to Christine; they exit, arm in arm

Granny and Nanny head for the exit

How much of my money's still left, Esme?

Granny Weatherwax Erm, well, not all that much, Gytha.

Nanny Ogg Oh well. Esme, how did you do it?

Granny Weatherwax What?

Nanny Ogg That trick with the sword. You did it. But you weren't hurt.

Granny Weatherwax I didn't have time. Not my fault.

Nanny Ogg One good thing, though. That blessed chandelier never came down. Looks too dramatic for its own good.

Granny Weatherwax Yes. That would have been too much. Even for opera.

Black-out

SCENE 17
Granny's Back Garden

Bird noise

Granny Weatherwax is digging a hole on stage. She has one of her hands bandaged. She pauses for a moment and sits on the edge of the hole

Granny Weatherwax Privies are good things, but you do need to move 'em around every now and then. You know where you are with a hole in the ground. It's uncomplicated. It's satisfying. What's more — after you've finished it, you can sit in the lovely warm knowledge that it'll be months before you'll need to do it again. Afternoon, Perdita. Come home for a visit, have you?

Agnes Nitt enters

Thought you were doing very well in the opera. Course, I'm not an expert on these things. Good to see young people seeking their fortune in the big city, though. When are you going back?

Agnes Nitt I — haven't decided.

Granny Weatherwax Weeelll, it doesn't pay to be always planning. Don't tie yourself down the whole time, I've always said that. Staying with your mam, are you?

Agnes Nitt Yes.

Granny Weatherwax Ah. Only Magrat's old cottage is still empty. You'd be doing everyone a favour if you aired it out a bit. You know — as long as you're here. (*Pause*) Funny ole thing, I wouldn't tell everyone, but I was only thinking the other day, about when I was younger and called myself Endemonidia ...

Agnes Nitt You did? When?

Granny Weatherwax Oh, for about three or four hours. Some names don't have the stayin' power. Never pick yourself a name you can't dig a new privy in. Give me a hand up, will you?

Agnes Nitt helps Granny Weatherwax to her feet

Time for a cup of tea? My, you are looking well. It's the fresh air. Too much stuffy air in that opera house, I thought.

Agnes Nitt Yes, I thought so too. Er — you've hurt your hand ...?

Granny Weatherwax It'll heal. A lot of things do. (*Pause*) This is just me askin', you understand, in a kind of neighbourly way, takin' an interest, sort of thing, wouldn't be human if I didn't.

Agnes Nitt (*with a sigh*) Yes?

Granny Weatherwax You got much to do with your evenings these days?

Agnes Nitt (*bridling slightly*) Oh? Are you offering to teach me something?

Granny Weatherwax Teach? Lord, no. Ain't got the patience for teaching. But I might let you learn.

They head for the exit together

Isn't this nice.

Black-out

FURNITURE AND PROPERTY LIST

ACT I

Phantom: lantern
Walter Plinge: broom
Mrs Plinge: box of wine bottles
Mr Arno: clipboard
Bat
Small "fire"
Mugs of tea for **Granny Weatherwax** and **Nanny Ogg**
Granny Weatherwax and **Nanny Ogg**: toasting forks
Big wodge of letters (in **Nanny Ogg**'s pocket)
Book: The Joye of Snacks (in **Nanny Ogg**'s pocket)
Mr Pounder: sack
Granny Weatherwax: broomstick and bags
Nanny Ogg: cat box, broom, bags, handbag containing purse full of coins, mirror, peppermints, grubby hanky
Chairs
Passenger: bottle opener
Desk
Ledgers
Tea things
Salzella: note
André: dark lantern (*practical*)
Agnes Nitt: glass of water, lighted candle
Christine: lighted candle
Bed
Large mirror
Nanny Ogg: paper
Señor Basilica: two opera tickets
Stagehands: pots of paint, pieces of scenery
Pounder's "legs"
Death of Rats: small scythe
Seldom Bucket: letter
Salzella: letter
Goatberger: large cut-out display board
"Harmonium"
Dr Underschaft: handkerchief
Nanny Ogg: Greebo cat
Walter Plinge: posters and paste pot
Seldom Bucket: watch
Woman with Chocs: box of chocolates, programme
Mrs Plinge: tray of drinks

ACT II

Sheet
Jar of pickled walnuts for **Nanny Ogg**
Mug of warm milk for **Agnes Nitt**
Christine: bouquet of flowers
Walter Plinge: more flowers
André: theatre programmes
Walter Plinge: letters
Agnes Nitt: candle
Walter Plinge: sack and lantern
Stagehands: table and chairs
Cutlery and food from main course of meal; pudding bowls and spoons, water jug
Nanny Ogg: chocolate pudding
Enrico Basilica: hanky
André: loose sheet music
Salzella: silver-topped sword-stick
Walter Plinge: bucket
Nanny Ogg: tray of drinks
Nanny Ogg: second tray of drinks, including a milk
Champagne bottle
Mrs Plinge: dustpan and brush
Piles of papers
Small organ
Music manuscripts
Lighted candles
Masks
Weapons
Shields
Nanny Ogg: sack of money
Salzella: knife
Agnes Nitt: ledgers
Items of scenery
André: police badge
Walter Plinge: sword in broom
Music (in **Nanny Ogg** 's pocket)
Granny Weatherwax: spade

LIGHTING PLOT

Practical fittings required: chandelier

ACT I

To open: Darkness; house lights up

Cue 1	Overture *Bring house lights down*	(Page 1)
Cue 2	Overture ends *Bring up follow spot on* **Phantom** *on balcony*	(Page 1)
Cue 3	**Phantom** exits *Cut follow spot; illuminate chandelier; bring up general interior lighting*	(Page 1)
Cue 4	The **Phantom** appears on the balcony *Cross-fade lights to blasted heath setting, with lightning; bring up pin spot on "fire"*	(Page 5)
Cue 5	The small curtains close *Cross-fade lights to general interior lighting*	(Page 9)
Cue 6	**Salzell**a strides off *Black-out*	(Page 12)
Cue 7	When ready *Bring up tight spotlight on* **Granny Weatherwax** *and* **Nanny Ogg**	(Page 13)
Cue 8	**Granny Weatherwax**: " ... just have a word with you?" *Black-out*	(Page 14)
Cue 9	Agonized cry *Bring up lights on stagecoach setting*	(Page 14)
Cue 10	**Nanny Ogg**: "... anybody got a bottle of beer?" *Black-out*	(Page 14)
Cue 11	When ready *Bring up lights on* **Mr Bucket**'s *office setting*	(Page 14)

Cue 12	**Salzella**: "Ah, opera!"	(Page 18)
	Black-out	
Cue 13	When ready	(Page 18)
	Bring up lights on stagecoach setting	
Cue 14	**Nanny Ogg**: "Come on, Esme."	(Page 20)
	Black-out	
Cue 15	**Agnes** enters	(Page 20)
	Covering spot on candle	
Cue 16	**André** opens the door in his lantern	(Page 20)
	*Bring up squared-off spot on **Agnes Nitt** to supplement practical lantern*	
Cue 17	**André** exits	(Page 21)
	Cut spot	
Cue 18	**Christine** enters	(Page 21)
	Bring up covering spot on candle	
Cue 19	**Christine** and **Agnes Nitt** exit	(Page 21)
	*Cut spots on candles; bring up light on **Christine**'s room*	
Cue 20	**The Phantom**: " ... how to sing it perfectly——"	(Page 21)
	Fade to black-out	
Cue 21	When ready	(Page 22)
	Bring up lights on inn interior setting	
Cue 22	The cat box rattles	(Page 23)
	Special lighting effects; strobe?	
Cue 23	**Nanny Ogg**: "Ooza ickle-wickle, then?"	(Page 23)
	Black-out	
Cue 24	When ready	(Page 24)
	Bring up lights on stagecoach setting	
Cue 25	**Nanny Ogg**: " — and stages."	(Page 25)
	Black-out	
Cue 26	When ready	(Page 25)
	Bring up lights on general interior setting	
Cue 27	**Mrs Plinge**: "Mr Pounder?"	(Page 27)
	Black-out	

Cue 28	**Mrs Plinge** exits *Bring up lights on balcony alone*	(Page 27)
Cue 29	**Mr Pounder**: "Squeak!" *Black-out*	(Page 28)
Cue 30	When ready *Bring up lights on general interior setting*	(Page 28)
Cue 31	**Seldom Bucket** and **Salzella** exit *Black-out*	(Page 30)
Cue 32	When ready *Bring up lights on publisher's office setting*	(Page 30)
Cue 33	**Nanny Ogg**, **Granny Weatherwax** and **Goatberger** exit *Black-out*	(Page 31)
Cue 34	When ready *Bring up lights on general interior setting*	(Page 32)
Cue 35	**Salzella** and **Seldom Bucket** exit *Cross-fade lights to balcony*	(Page 37)
Cue 36	**Nanny Ogg** and **Granny Weatherwax** sit *Dim balcony lights; bring up lights from "stage"*	(Page 38)
Cue 37	**Granny Weatherwax**: " ... this place is a maze!" *Change lights to corridor setting*	(Page 40)
Cue 38	**Nanny Ogg**: " ... fifteen minutes, though, please." *Black-out*	(Page 41)

ACT II

To open: Darkness

Cue 39	Scream *Bring up general interior lighting*	(Page 42)
Cue 41	**Nanny Ogg**: "Miraculous recovery, that. Not." *Black-out*	(Page 45)
Cue 41	When ready *Bring up lighting for dark, threatening street scene*	(Page 45)

Cue 42   **Granny Weatherwax**: "Let's do some good."   (Page 46)
             Black-out

Cue 43   When ready   (Page 47)
             Bring up lights on balcony

Cue 44   **Granny Weatherwax**: "What is it you've seen?"   (Page 48)
             Black-out

Cue 45   When ready   (Page 49)
             Bring up lights on bedroom setting

Cue 46   **Phantom**: "The Man of a Thousand Faces" ... Music   (Page 50)
             Black-out

Cue 47   When ready   (Page 50)
             Bring up general interior lighting

Cue 48   **Agnes Nitt**: "Hallo, André."   (Page 51)
             Fade lights slightly on **Salzella** *and* **Seldom Bucket**
                 and brighten lights slightly on **Agnes Nitt** *an*d **André**

Cue 49   **André** passes **Salzella** and **Seldom Bucket**   (Page 52)
             Brighten lights on **Salzella** *and* **Seldom Bucket**

Cue 50   **Granny Weatherwax**: "Only the one on the outside."   (Page 54)
             Black-out

Cue 51   When ready   (Page 54)
             Bring up lights on office setting

Cue 52   **Enrico Basilica**, **Granny Weatherwax** and
                 Nanny Ogg *exchange winks*   (Page 56)
             Black-out

Cue 53   When ready   (Page 56)
             Bring up gloomy cellar lighting with water effect

Cue 54   **Agnes** enters with a candle   (Page 56)
             Bring up covering spot on candle

Cue 55   **Agnes Nitt**: "Come on, Greebo." They exit   (Page 57)
             Black-out

Cue 56   When ready   (Page 57)
             Bring up lights on office setting

Cue 57	**Granny Weatherwax**: "At the moment, yes." *Black-out*	(Page 61)
Cue 58	When ready *Bring up general interior lighting*	(Page 61)
Cue 59	**Agnes Nitt**: "Come on, Christine." *Black-out*	(Page 64)
Cue 60	When ready *Bring up general interior lighting*	(Page 64)
Cue 61	**Salzella**: "Now come on." *Black-out*	(Page 67)
Cue 62	When ready *Bring up lights on corridor setting*	(Page 67)
Cue 63	**Nanny Ogg**: " ... deserve to bounce." *Black-out*	(Page 69)
Cue 64	When ready *Bring up "glow from stage" on balcony*	(Page 69)
Cue 65	**Walter Plinge** enters *Bring up spot outside the balcony*	(Page 69)
Cue 66	**Greebo** follows **Walter Plinge** over the rail *Cross-fade lights to general setting*	(Page 70)
Cue 67	**Agnes Nitt** protests ad lib *Cross-fade lights to Opera House roof setting, 　with star gobo on background*	(Page 71)
Cue 68	A small crowd enters *Bring up lights on "ground level"*	(Page 72)
Cue 69	**Nanny Ogg** starts to enter the trapdoor *Black-out*	(Page 73)
Cue 70	**Voices**: "Come back, you coward!" *etc.* *Bring up lights dimly*	(Page 73)
Cue 71	**Granny Weatherwax**: "Go on!" *Black-out*	(Page 76)

Cue 72   When ready   (Page 76)
                  Bring up lights on **Phantom**'s *lair*

Cue 73   **Nanny Ogg** exits   (Page 77)
                  Black-out; bring up light in balcony

Cue 74   The **Phantom** saws the rope   (Page 77)
                  Black-out

Cue 75   When ready   (Page 77)
                  Bring up general interior lighting

Cue 76   **Granny Weatherwax** and **André** exit   (Page 79)
                  Cross-fade lights to balcony

Cue 77   They all exit   (Page 80)
                  Black-out

Cue 78   When ready   (Page 80)
                  Bring up lights on **Phantom**'s *lair*

Cue 79   **Granny Weatherwax**: "Let's do some good!"   (Page 81)
                  Black-out

Cue 80   Tenor aria is interrupted   (Page 81)
                  Bring up general interior lighting

Cue 81   Dramatic chord   (Page 82)
                  Change lighting to highlight Walter's entrance

Cue 82   **Granny Weatherwax**: "Even for opera."   (Page 86)
                  Black-out

Cue 83   When ready   (Page 87)
                  Bring up lights on back garden setting

Cue 84   **Granny Weatherwax**: "Isn't this nice."   (Page 88)
                  Black-out

EFFECTS PLOT

ACT I

Cue 13	**Dr Underschaft**: "Good-morning, Perdita, how are you?" **Agnes Nitt**'s *voice over speakers, "live"*	(Page 32)
Cue 14	**Dr Underschaft**: "... run through it. André?" *Introduction on harmonium,* **Dr Underschaft**'s *voice,* *singing*	(Page 32)
Cue 15	**André** stops playing *Cut harmonium and singing*	(Page 32)
Cue 16	**Dr Underschaft**: " ... as Christine would sing it, hmm?" *Introduction on harmonium,* **Christine**'s *voice, singing*	(Page 32)
Cue 17	**André** stops playing *Cut harmonium and singing*	(Page 32)
Cue 18	**Dr Underschaft**: " ... it ought to be sung?" *Introduction on harmonium,* **Agnes**'s *voice, singing.* *When finished, cut live microphone*	(Page 32)
Cue 19	**Nanny Ogg**: " ... organ, young man." **Voice**: (*taped or on live microphone, running up a scale*) "La, la, la .." *and continuing, stopping before next cue*	(Page 35)
Cue 20	**Granny Weatherwax**: "Someone's singing. Listen." **Voice:** (*taped or on live microphone*): "*Doh, Re, Mi, Fah,* *So, La, Ti, Doh!*"	(Page 35)
Cue 21	Lights dim in the Gods *Distant music and singing*	(Page 38)
Cue 22	**Nanny Ogg**: " ... that's making all the noise." *Momentary lull in music*	(Page 39)
Cue 23	**Granny Weatherwax** and **Nanny Ogg** exit *Dialogue over speakers as p. 40*	(Page 40)
Cue 24	Lights change to corridor *Volume of music decreases*	(Page 40)
Cue 25	**Nanny Ogg** gives **Granny Weatherwax** a warning look *Music fades to silence*	(Page 41)
Cue 26	**Nanny** Ogg starts to drink the contents of the tray *Bells ring in boxes*	(Page 41)

ACT II

PROJECTION PLOT

ACT I

Cue 1   **Salzella** hands the note to **Seldom Bucket**   (Page 16)
Project note on screen; text p. 16

Cue 2   **Seldom Bucket** hands the letter to **Salzella**   (Page 28)
Project letter on screen; text p. 28

Cue 3   **Seldom Bucket** opens the second letter   (Page 28)
Project second letter on screen; text p. 28

ACT II

Cue 4   **Seldom Bucket**: "Mr Salzella!"   (Page 50)
Project letter on screen; text p. 50